FOUNDATIONS THAT SUSTAIN AMERICA

Foundations That Sustain America

DR. CHUCK HARDING

PASTOR T. MICHAEL CREED

First published in 2016 by Bible & Literature Missionary Foundation
a ministry of Victory Baptist Church, Shelbyville, TN 37160

Awake America Inc.
113 Second St. North East
Washington, D.C. 20002

Cover design by Alan Salway
Edited by Valerie Creed and Jo Harding
Special thanks to Pat Deason type-setting

Special thanks to the Library of Congress for their historic documentation.
The authors and publication team have put every effort to give proper
credit to quotes and thoughts that are not original with the authors.
It is not our intent to claim originality with any quote or
thought that could not readily be tied to an original source.

ISBN 978-0-9789325-1-0

ISBN 978-0-9789325-1-0

54000

9 780978 932510

Printed in the United States of America

Dedication

There is an old adage which states, *Behind every great man there is a great woman.* We make no pretense of being great men, but our wives have certainly been behind us in our endeavors for the glory of God, for the sake of the Gospel, and for the good of America. It is for this reason, we wish to dedicate this book to our wives, Jo Harding and Valerie Creed, who together have been essential in the composition of this book. Their tireless dedication has been a source of tremendous blessing to both of us. Their sacrificial spirit of themselves and of their time has brought to fruition *The Foundations That Sustain America.*

Proverbs 18:22 *Whoso findeth a wife findeth a good thing, and obtaineth favour of the Lord.*

Dr. Charles S. Harding
Pastor T. Michael Creed

Definition of Foundation

FOUNDA'TION, *noun* [Latin fundatio, fundo.]

The basis or ground work, or any thing; that on which any thing stands, and by which it is supported. A free government has its *foundation* in the choice and consent of the people to be governed. Christ is the *foundation* of the church.

1828 Webster's Dictionary

Contents

Preface

What an honor to complete our third book, *The Foundations That Sustain America*. During the authorship of this book, our desire was to do more than read and research; it was to listen to those architects of early America who laid her sure foundations upon the Stone, the tried Stone, that precious Corner Stone. These architects offered a personal sacrifice physically, spiritually, and financially speaking loudly by it as illustrated in Hebrews 11:4d, *he being dead yet speaketh*.

Our hopeful prayer is every person who picks up this book will do more than just read it; he or she will instead:

- Sit in the humble cottage of Wycliffe and watch as he and his protégés, paying meticulous attention to each and every detail, copy God's Word.

- Look over the shoulder of Johannes Gutenberg as he peers at the first page of the Bible from his printing press and watch with wonder as the common man reads his personal copy of the Holy Bible for the first time in his life.

- Sail with Columbus, smelling the salted air, and look as this great explorer's face, furling with concern, is changed into unspeakable joy when the words *Land Ho!* are shouted from the crow's nest at the first sight of the New World.

- Watch as the Founding Fathers in the hushed, freedom hall pick up a quill pen to sign that parchment declaring to the entire world men had God-given, inalienable rights.

- Listen to bold, brilliant, benevolent men risking their all as they dig deeply the foundations of the greatest nation in modern history; the United States of America.

May all who read this book be motivated to maintain *the foundations that sustain America.*

Isaiah 28:16 *Therefore thus saith the Lord God, Behold, I lay in Zion for a foundation a stone, a tried stone, a precious corner stone, a sure foundation: he that believeth shall not make haste.*

Dr. & Mrs. Charles S. Harding

My wife and I count it a privilege to have been a part of the research for *The Foundations That Sustain America.* We were as archeologists, as we studied, digging at an American, archeological site for the first time. As we explored deeper under the surface, we found artifacts that linked us to the early years of American history. Carried back in our minds to Ellis Island in the 1800s, we could almost hear the voices of the many immigrants desiring to make America their home. We stood on Cole's Hill as the Pilgrims buried their first deceased that initial winter and watched them wipe away tears of sorrow. We sat in the sitting-room of Mary Ball Washington's home while she read to her children and grandchildren. We knelt in prayer with her on her Prayer Rock and sensed her urgency as she prayed for her son during the War for Independence. Truly these were remarkable finds; comprising a sustaining foundation we will never forget.

Pastor and Mrs. T. Michael Creed

Chapter One

Foundations of the Fervent

Washington Monument

U.S. Capitol

Supreme Court

White House

Architectural foundations are used to bear the load of a structure or a building when it is lowered down through the upper, weaker layer of topsoil to the stronger layer of subsoil or bedrock below. There are different types of foundations with the oldest being wooden piles, then steel, reinforced concrete, or even pre-tensioned concrete. The higher or the heavier the structure, the deeper the foundation must be.

Improperly Laid Foundation

In world history, as in architecture, foundations are a necessity. Long before any civilization is established, a foundation must be laid and from this foundation the nation arises. If it is a deep foundation, the nation will stand; if it is a shallow, improperly-laid foundation that nation shall fail and shall fall over a period of time. This truth has been illustrated in the annuals of history over and over again when nations have risen and nations have fallen, and great has been their destruction. This truth is illustrated in the Holy Bible.

Luke 6:47-49 *Whosoever cometh to me, and heareth my sayings, and doeth them, I will shew you to whom he is like: He is like a man which built an house, and digged deep, and laid the foundation on a rock:and when the flood arose, the stream beat vehemently upon that house, and could not shake it: for it was founded upon a rock. But he that heareth, and doeth not, is like a man that without a foundation built an house upon the earth; against which the stream did beat vehemently, and immediately it fell; and the ruin of that house was great.*

John Wycliffe

The ground breaking for the United States of America began in the 1300s when John Wycliffe began translating the Bible into the common man's tongue and began training his students to propagate the Gospel of Jesus Christ throughout Europe. Because every Bible had to be hand copied, the progress was slow. During the 14th and 15th centuries it seemed human progress came to a screeching halt. There were no advancements in natural science, and learning along with university attendance were in decline. Violence, lawlessness, and poverty were common place in the era, and wars and conflicts between countries and families were the norm. These conflicts were not economically motivated but were born out of man's darker character, man's hatred and his vengeance. Wars were rampant, city-state against city-state, region against region, nation against nation; a societal condition that resulted in the preponderance of famine, poverty and misery. Human rights were almost non-existent; brutality and devastation were customary with shocking mass destruction prevalent everywhere.

EDWARD IV.

England's King Edward the Fourth instituted the use of torture for both the accused and for their witnesses in judicial proceedings; a practice that would continue for over two centuries. Even more disturbing was the fact that the public had degenerated into such cruelty that they enjoyed the public torture and executions even cheering when someone was drawn and quartered or cheering during other forms of public humiliation. Torture brought ovations of delight from all onlookers. Poverty was widespread with thousands of houses being empty and with tens of thousands begging for food in the streets. Corn and potatoes were unknown to Europeans at this time; meat was scarce, and meals were sparse, if existent at all. Cities were catalysts for contagions; if famine did not kill you, a variety of diseases would.

Bubonic plague, called the *Black Death*, was killing millions throughout Europe, and in England one out of every three people died from this plague. We still sing the childhood song, *Ring around the rosies, Pocket full of posies, Ashes! Ashes! We all fall down*. This song has been handed down through history with many thinking it represented this time in Europe. A red, rose spot would have appeared on the skin when you had contracted the plague, and people thought posies, a type of flower, would ward off the plague so they carried posies in their pockets. *We all fall down* describes the fact of the millions who died. One historian wrote, *There will not be enough men left to bury the dead; nor the means to dig enough graves. So many corpses will lie in the houses.*

Another noted historian wrote, *A general feeling of impending calamity hangs over all. Perpetual danger prevails everywhere.*

Because of no spiritual truth, the collapse of morality was commonplace. Treachery, betrayal, corruption, debauchery, prostitution, and adultery were wide-spread making the end of the world seriously contemplated by the European mind. Discouragement and despair were everywhere you looked. This age of darkness and ignorance had lasted for centuries, but then several things occurred that changed the course of human history. In the 1400s two very significant events occurred.

Johannes Gutenberg

Page of the
Gutenberg Bible

Gutenberg Press

The first relates to a young boy, Johannes, who used to play in his father's workshop. As his father, who was a scribe, meticulously copied manuscripts, Johannes entertained himself by carving his initials in blocks of wood and then by setting them on a table. During the course of a particular day, one of the blocks fell off the table and into a pail of purple dye causing Johannes to quickly pluck it from the pail and put it on a piece of paper to dry. As he picked it up from the paper, he saw it left a perfect image on the paper, and the idea of the printing press began to germinate in his mind. Twenty years later Johannes Gutenberg gave us the first printing press with movable type in Western civilization. Gutenberg's introduction of moveable-type printing to Europe played a key role in sharing of knowledge throughout the land and in laying the material basis for a knowledge-based economy and the advanced development of science in the European culture. This knowledge spread to all European humanity. In the 1450s the Gutenberg Bible was printed and the common man began reading God's Word and began finding the truth of the Gospel which caused many to receive Jesus Christ as LORD and Savior.

The second significant event occurred four decades later when Columbus set sail on his historic voyage to find a better route to the West Indies, but what he found was the New World. The discovery of America impacted the Old World in amazing ways for what commenced in Europe with Columbus' discovery, commenced to formulate an opened door the foundations of the United States of America. The Old World was about to become the recipient of new types of food stuffs, of amazing assortment of precious metals, of timber in abundance to build better dwellings and to build stronger ships. There were also a wide array of animal furs to keep the body warm, and other sources of wealth and resources from the New World that revived the European economy.

Of all these changes, the most important change was about to unfold, and it was not of a material kind. For centuries the minds and hearts of mankind were chained in darkness and ignorance. Bibles had been "locked up" to Latin only to be read by the few because the common man was told he would not be able to understand the Bible. Because of Gutenberg's printing press, the Bible was available to the common man in his own language. Men began to be brought up in the nurture and admonition of the Word of God, the Holy Bible.

The Europeans began to realize man had a right to worship under the dictates of his own heart. They also began to understand the God Who gave them life, also gave them liberty; that mankind had a right to live freely and had a right to pursue that which motivated him not because the government or the monarchy said so, but because his God had given him these rights. With the New World now available and with the generations being infused with these truths, by the 1600s mankind was about to embark upon one of the most amazing ventures in the history of the world; the birth of a new nation conceived in liberty and founded upon the principles of the Holy Bible and pioneered by faithful followers who were looking for a nation *whose Builder and Maker was God.*

These faithful followers were the Separatists who actually referred to themselves as the *Saints*. They found religious freedom in Holland but the secular life was more than they could bear. The craft guilds were closed to foreigners making it hard for the men to care for their families as they were only afforded low and menial positions. Holland had an opened society which was very attractive to the Separatists children who were being drawn away into this society so the decision was made to travel to the New World enabling the establishment of a colony that would have no worldly influence or governmental interference. (This would be likened today with colonizing the moon!) After returning to London, they received permission to found a settlement on the East Coast of the New World in Virginia. Because of the delay of the leaky *Speedwell* the trip was delayed. The new embarkation in September coincided with the worst of the storm seasons in European waters from the southern port of England interestingly called *Plymouth*. The crossing to the New World was beyond unpleasant, was treacherous, and was without privacy especially for the women of whom several were pregnant. Even with these challenges, the Pilgrim Forefathers reached their destination and laid the beginning of the first foundations for their new country which was miraculous in its inception, Biblical in its design, and unique in its longevity.

George Washington, the *Father of America*, had a great deal to say about the founding of his country. The following excerpts are submitted for your edification:

The foundational days of the United States of America find clarity in the papers of George Washington. At his death, these papers which filled more than two hundred, folio volumes were bequeathed to Washington's nephew, Bushrod Washington. The Congress of the United States later purchased these papers and had them deposited in the National Archives. The family of Washington favored a Mr. Sparks, a well-known editor at the time, to compile these papers into twelve, large octavo-volumes, adorned with portraits, plates, and fac-similes, under the title of *The Writings of George Washington*. Mr. Sparks also traveled over America and Europe seeking for any documents necessary to illustrate and to complete this authentic biography of George Washington.

In 1838, when this work had just been completed, the American editor applied to M. Guizot, an author and statesman in France, to review his work and to make selections in writing from a European point of view. Mr. Guizot's *Essay on the Character and Influence of Washington in the Revolution of the United States of America* was written in French with his second edition being translated into English in 1863.
(New York: Published by James Miller, 522 Broadway. 1863)

National Archives

p. 13

...If there were ever a just cause, and one which deserved success, it was that of the English colonies in their struggle to become the United States of America. In their case, open insurrection had been preceded by resistance. This resistance was founded upon historical right and upon facts, upon natural right and upon opinions.

It is the honorable distinction of England to have given to her colonies, in their infancy, the seminal principle of their liberty. Almost all of them, either at the time of their being planted or shortly after, received charters which conferred upon the colonists the rights of the mother country. And these charters were not a mere deceptive form, a dead letter, for they either established or recognized those powerful institutions which impelled the colonists to defend their liberties and to control power by dividing it; such as the laying of taxes by vote, the election of the principal public bodies, trial by jury, and the right to meet and deliberate upon affairs of general interest.

p. 16

At the same time with their legal rights, the colonists had also religious faith. It was not only as Englishmen, but as Christians, that they wished to be free; and their faith was more dear to them than their charters. Indeed, these charters were, in their eyes, nothing more than a manifestation and an image, however imperfect, of the great law of God, the Gospel. Their rights would not have been lost, even had they been deprived of their charters. In their enthusiastic state of mind, supported by divine favor, they would have traced these rights to a source superior and inaccessible to all human power; for they cherished sentiments more elevated than even the institutions themselves, over which they were so sensitively watchful...

p. 17

...Philosophical opinions were there combined with religious belief, the triumphs of reason with the heritage of faith, and the rights of man with those of the Christian.

p. 18

...For religious belief promotes, to an incalculable extent, the wise management of human affairs. In order to discharge properly the duty assigned to him in this life,

man must contemplate it from a higher point of view; if his mind be merely on the same level with the task he is performing, he will soon fall below it, and become incapable of accomplishing it in a worthy manner.

*Such was the fortunate condition, both of man and of society, in the English colonies, when, in a spirit of haughty aggression, **England undertook to control their fortunes and their destiny, without their own consent...***

pp. 19-20

...In the infancy of the English colonies, three different powers are found, side by side with their liberties, and consecrated by the same charters,--the crown, the proprietary founders, whether companies or individuals, and the mother country. The crown, by virtue of the monarchical principle, and with its traditions, derived from the Church and the Empire. The proprietary founders, to whom the territory had been granted, by virtue of the feudal principal, which attaches a considerable portion of sovereignty to the proprietorship of the soil. The mother country, by virtue of the colonial principle, which, at all periods and among all nations, by a natural connexion between facts and opinions, has given to the mother country a great influence over the population proceeding from its bosom.

From the very commencement, as well in the course of events as in the charters, there was great confusion among these various powers...

p. 23

...Moreover, it was henceforth not the crown alone, but the crown and the mother country united, with which the colonies had to deal. Their real sovereign was no longer the king, but the king and the people of Great Britain, represented and mingled together in Parliament...

In the mean time, the colonies were rapidly increasing in population, in wealth, in strength internally, and in importance externally. Instead of a few obscure establishments, solely occupied with their own affairs, and hardly able to sustain their own existence, a people was now forming itself...

pp. 24-26

...The mother country, unable to govern them well, had neither the leisure nor the ill will to oppress them absolutely. She vexed and annoyed them without checking their growth...As early as 1692, the General Court of Massachusetts passed a resolution "that no tax should be levied upon his Majesty's subjects in the colonies, without the consent of the Governor and Council, and the representatives in General Court assembled."

GEORGE the III.

...Thus, when that day arrived, when George the Third and his Parliament, rather in a spirit of pride, and to prevent the loss of absolute power by long disuse, than to derive any advantage from its exercise, undertook to tax the colonies without their consent, a powerful, numerous, and enthusiastic party,-- the national party,--immediately sprang into being, ready to resist, in the name of right and of national honor.

It was indeed a question of right and of honor, and not of interest or physical well-being. The taxes were light, and imposed no burden upon the colonists. But they belonged to that class of men who feel most keenly the wrongs which affect the mind alone, and who can find no repose while honor is unsatisfied. "For, Sir, what is it we are contending against? Is it against paying the duty of three pence per pound on tea, because burdensome? No; it is the right only, that we have all along disputed." (Washington to Bryan Fairfax. Washington's Writings, Vol. II. P. 392) Such was, at the commencement of the quarrel, the language of Washington himself, and such was the public sentiment—a sentiment founded in sound policy, as well as moral sense, and manifesting as much judgment as virtue...

Benjamin Franklin in London Presenting the Concerns of the American Colonists

pp. 30-32

...Insurrection, resistance to established authority, and the enterprise of forming a new government, are matters of grave importance to men like these, to all men of sense and virtue. Those who have the most forecast, never calculate its whole extent. The boldest would shudder in their hearts, could they foresee all the dangers of the undertaking. Independence was not the premeditated purpose, not even the wish, of the colonies. A few bold and sagacious spirits either saw that it would come, or expressed their desire for it, after the period of resistance under the forms of law had passed. But the American people did not aspire to it, and did not urge their leaders to make claim to it. "'For all what you Americans say of your loyalty,' observed the illustrious Lord Camden, at that time Mr. Pratt, 'I know you will one day throw off your dependence upon this country; and, notwithstanding your boasted affection to it, will set up for independence.' Franklin answered, 'No such idea is entertained in the minds of the Americans; and no such idea will ever enter their heads, unless you grossly abuse them.' 'Very true,' replied Mr. Pratt, 'that is one of the main causes I see will happen, and will produce the event.'"
(*Washington's Writings*, Vol. II. P. 496)

Charles Pratt, Lord Camden

Lord Camden was right in his conjectures. English America was grossly abused; and yet, in 1774, and even in 1775, hardly a year before the declaration of independence, and when it was becoming inevitable, Washington and Jefferson thus wrote; "Although you are taught, I say, to believe, that the people of Massachusetts are rebellious, setting up for independency, and what not, give me leave, my good friend, to tell you, that you are abused, grossly abused...I can announce it as a fact, that it is not the wish or interest of that government, or any other upon this continent, separately or collectively, to set up for independence; but this you may, at the same time, rely on, that none of them will ever submit to the loss of those valuable rights and privileges, which are essential to the happiness of every free state, and without which, life, liberty, and property are rendered totally insecure." (Letter to Robert Mackenzie, 9 October, 1774; Washington's Writings, Vol. II. P. 400) "Believe me, dear Sir, there is not in the British empire a man, who more cordially loves a union with Great Britain than I do. But, by the God that made me, I will cease to exist, before I will yield to a connexion on such terms as the British Parliament propose, and, in this, I think I speak the sentiments of America. We want neither inducement nor power to declare and assert a separation. It is will alone, which is wanting, and that is growing apace, under the fostering hand of our King." (Letter to Mr. Randolph, 29th November, 1775; Jefferson's Memoirs and Correspondence, Vol. I. p. 153)

...In vain were fresh petitions constantly presented to him (King George), *always loyal and respectful without insincerity; in vain was his name commended to the favor and protection of God, in the services of religion, according to usual custom. He paid no attention...to the prayers...which were offered to Heaven in his behalf; and by his order the war continued, without ability, without vigorous and well-combined efforts, but with that hard and haughty obstinacy, which destroys in the heart all affection as well as hope.*

Evidently the day had arrived, when power had forfeited its claim to loyal obedience; and when the people were called upon to protect themselves by force, no longer finding in the established order of things either safety or shelter. Such a moment is a fearful one, big with unknown events; one, which no human sagacity can predict, and no human government can control, but which, notwithstanding, does sometimes come, bearing an impress stamped by the hand of God. If the struggle, which begins at such a moment, were one absolutely forbidden; it, at the mysterious point in which it arises, this great social duty did not press even upon the heads of those who deny its existence, the human race, long ago, wholly fallen under the yoke, would have lost all dignity as well as all happiness...

Parliament Building, London

pp. 35-36

...eloquent voices were constantly lifted up, in the British Parliament itself, in support of the colonies and of their rights. This is the glory and distinction of a representative government, that it insures to every cause its champions, and brings even into the arena of politics those defences, which were instituted for the sanctuary of the laws.

Europe, moreover, could not be a passive spectator of such a struggle. Two great powers, France and Spain, had serious losses and recent injuries in America itself, to avenge upon England...Holland could not fail to assist America, against her ancient rival, with her capital, and her credit...

...every thing united and acted in concert in favor of the insurgent colonies. Their cause was just, their strength already great, and their characters marked by prudence and morality...

Washington Praying

p. 61

...Nine years were to be spent in war to obtain independence, and ten years in political discussion to form a system of government. Obstacles, reverses, enmities, treachery, mistakes, public indifference, personal antipathies; all these incumbered the progress of Washington, during this long period. But his faith and hope were never shaken for a moment. In the darkest hours, when he was obliged to contend against the sadness which hung upon his own spirits, he says, "...I do not believe, that Providence has done so much for nothing...The great Governor of the universe has led us too long and too far on the road to happiness and glory to forsake us in the midst of it..." (*Washington's Writings*, Vol. IX, pp. 5, 383, 392)

George Washington's Papers
at the Library of Congress

George Washington to Meshech Weare
et al, June 8, 1783
Circular Letter of Farewell to the Army

I now make it my earnest prayer, that God would have you...to entertain a brotherly affection and love for one another, for their fellow Citizens of the United States at large, and particularly for their brethren who have served in the Field, and finally, that he would most graciously be pleased to dispose us all, to do Justice, to love mercy, and to demean ourselves with that Charity, humility, and pacific temper of mind, which were the Characteristicks of the Divine Author of our Blessed Religion, and without an humble imitation of whose example in these things, we can never hope to be a happy Nation.

Chapter Two

Foundations of the Forefathers

The Mayflower Compact, 1620

As the chilling winds of November iced the *Mayflower*, forty-one Pilgrims within her cabin were signing the Mayflower Compact in the year 1620. The Pilgrims having acquired a patent from the Virginia Company of London needed this document because the *Mayflower* was forced to make landfall not in Virginia but in the newly renamed land of New England, previously known as the Northern Parts of Virginia. Thirteen years earlier, in 1607, the Virginia Company of London had sent 104 English men and boys under her patent to establish Jamestown

Ruins of the Old Brick Church at Jamestown

in Virginia, but three years later, in 1610, eighty to ninety percent of them had died due to starvation and disease. Their colony had the sole purpose of entrepreneurs looking for financial gain, whereas, the Pilgrims' sole purpose was a group of Separatists looking for religious freedom; being only governed by the laws of Christ as stated in the New Testament of the Holy Bible. The Virginia Company of London had granted permission for English settlers to write governing documents like the Mayflower Compact as stated in the Company's ruling passed on February 2, 1620: *that such Captains and Leaders of particular Plantations that shall go there to inhabit by virtue of their Grants, and plant themselves, their tenants and servants in Virginia, shall have liberty, till a form of Government be here settled for them, associating with them divers of the gravest and discreetest of their Companies, to make Order, Ordinances and Constitutions for the better ordering and directing of their servants and business, provided they be not repugnant to the Laws of England. (Records of Virginia Company, Vol. I)* The Pilgrims knowing they had staked their lives upon a venture for religious freedom readily disembarked the *Mayflower* with their new governing document, the Mayflower Compact, in their grasp. The Mayflower Compact was copied and sent back with the *Mayflower* on her return journey to England in April of 1621. What was the significance of this Compact? What kind of effect did the Compact have on America?

Any time a new foundation is laid, strengthening elements are considered. There is a search for stable ground and a search for solid materials which will reinforce the foundation throughout the passing of time. The Mayflower Compact, along with the first assembling of a representative-legislative body in America known as the House of Burgesses in 1619 Jamestown, and other actions taken by American Forefathers have sustained America's foundation through the many storms she has faced. We will examine several of the first foundations that were laid particularly by the determined Pilgrim Fathers of Plymouth Colony; their Mayflower Compact, their first steps onto Plymouth Rock, their burial sites, and the *National Monument to the Forefathers*.

The Mayflower

The Mayflower Compact

Others had joined the *Mayflower* in her journey who were not Separatists. These were the discontent and mutinous among them. Governor William Bradford best lays out the reasoning for the Mayflower Compact in his journal, *Of Plimoth Plantation 1620-1647*. (2. Booke).

...

I shall a litle returne backe and begine with a combination made by them before they came ashore, being ye first foundation of their govermente in this place; occasioned partly by ye discontented & mutinous speeches that some of the strangers amongst them had let fall from them in ye ship—That when they came a shore they would use their owne libertie; for none had power to comand them, the patente they had being for Virginia, and not for New-england, which belonged to an other Goverment, with which ye Virginia Company had nothing to doe. And partly that shuch an acte by them done (this their condition considered) might be as firme as any patent, and in some respects more sure.

The forme was as followeth.

In ye name of God, Amen. We whose names are underwriten, they loyall subjects of our dread soveraigne Lord, King James, by ye grace of God, of Great Britaine, Franc, & Ireland king, defender of ye faith, &c., haveing undertaken, for ye glorie of God, and advancemente of ye Christian faith, and honour of our king & countrie, a voyage to plant ye first colonie in ye Northerne parts of Virginia, doe by these presents solemnly & mutualy in ye presence of God, and one of another, covenant & combine our selves togeather into a civill body politick, for our better ordering & preservation & furtherance of ye ends aforesaid; and by virtue hearof to enacte, constitute, and frame such just & equall lawes, ordinances, acts, constitutions, & offices, from time to time, as shall be thought most meete & convenient for ye generall good of ye Colonie, unto which we promise all due submission and obedience. In witness wherof we have hereunder subscribed our names at Cap-Codd ye 11. of November, in ye year of ye raigne of our soveraigne lord, King James, of England, France, & Ireland ye eighteenth, and of Scotland ye fiftie fourth. An°: Dom. 1620.

After this they chose, or rather confirmed, M(r). John Carver (a man godly & well approved amongst them) their Governour for that year. And after they had provided a place for their goods, or comone store, (Which were long in unlading for want of boats, foulness of winter weather, and sicknes of diverce,) and begune some small cottages for their habitation, as time would admitte, they mette and consulted of lawes & orders, both for their civill & military Govermente, as ye necessitie of their condition did require, still adding thereunto as urgent occasion in severall times, and as cases did require.

In these hard & difficulte beginings they found some discontents & murmurings arise amongst some, and mutinous speeches & carriags in other: but they were soone quelled & overcome by ye wisdom, patience, and just & equall carrage of things by ye Gov(r) and better part, w(ch) clave faithfully togeather in ye maine.

The passengers of the *Mayflower* are listed in Bradford's journal but the signers of the Mayflower Compact are not designated. The original Compact has since disappeared, but we assume Nathaniel Morton had access to it. We look to Nathaniel Morton's *New Englands Memoriall* (1669) for the list of signers. In Morton's Epistle Dedicatory in his book, he writes, *The greatest part of my intelligence hath been borrowed from my much honored Uncle, Mr. William Bradford, and such Manuscripts as he left in his study, from the year 1620 unto 1646.* (p. 12)

Edward Winslow

The signers of the Mayflower Compact are as follows: *John Carver, John Howland, William Brewster, Edward Winslow, George Soule, William Bradford, Isaac Allerton, Samuel Fuller, *John Crackston, Myles Standish, *Christopher Martin, *William Mullins, *William White, Stephen Hopkins, Edward Doty, Edward Lester, Richard Warren, John Billington, *Edward Tilley, *John Tilley, Francis Cooke, *Thomas Rogers, *Thomas Tinker, *John Rigsdale, *James Chilton, *Edward Fuller, *John Turner, *Francis Eaton, *Moses Fletcher, *John Goodman, *Thomas Williams, *Digory Priest, *Edmund Margesson, Peter Browne, *Richard Britteridge, *Richard Clarke, Richard Gardiner, Gilbert Winslow, John Alden, *John Allerton, and *Thomas English.

*These all died the first winter or shortly after coming ashore from the *Mayflower*.

As you read the Mayflower Compact, you will notice some key ingredients to the success of the Plymouth colony. First we see the Compact beginning with, *In ye name of God, Amen*. It also states...*having undertaken, for ye glorie of God, and advancement of ye Christian faith*. They affirmed...*these presents solemnly & mutualy in ye presence of God, and one of another, covenant & combine our selves togeather into a civill body politick*. They recognized God as their Supreme Authority and as the One Who was ever watching. We see next they were sincerely interested in true liberty of the individual...*to enact, constitute, and frame such just & equall lawes, ordinances, acts, constitutions, & offices*. They were mutually committed to working together for the good of all...*as shall be thought most meete & convenient for ye general good of ye Colonie, unto which we promise all due submission and obedience*. Last, we notice these signers were surrendered to the cause by ascribing their names to the Compact...*In witness wherof we have hereunder subscribed our names at Cap-Codd ye 11. of November*.

An example of "an equal law established" was agreed on after their first winter was over in Plymouth. It is found in Bradford's *Of Plimoth Plantation 1620-1647*, chapter fourteen.

...At length, after much debate of things, the Gov(r) with ye advise of ye cheefest amongst them gave way that they should set corne every man for his owne perticuler, and in that regard trust to them selves; in all other things to goe on in ye generall way as before. And so assigned to every family a parcell of land, according to the proportion of their number for that end, only for present use (but made no devission for inheritance), and ranged all boys & youth under some familie. This had very good success, for it made all hands very industrious, so as much more corne was planted then other waise would have bene by any means ye Gov(r) or any other could use, and saved him a great deall of trouble, and gave farr better contente. The women now wente willingly into ye feild, and tooke their litl-ons with them to set corne, which before would aledg weaknes, and inabilitie; whom to have compelled would have bene thought great tiranie and oppression.

The experience that was had in this comone course and condition, tried sundrie years, and that amongst godly and sober men, may well evince the vanitie of that conceite of Platos & other ancients, applauded by some of later times;--that ye taking away of propertie, and bringing in comunitie into a comone welath, would make them happy and florishing; as if they were wiser than God...

The Mayflower Compact was one of the foundational documents for America. John Quincy Adams stated in 1802, *This is perhaps the only instance in human history of that positive, original social compact which speculative philosophers have imagined as the only legitimate source of government. Here was a unanimous and personal assent by all the individuals of the community to the association, "by which they became a nation"...the settlers of all the former European colonies had contented themselves with the powers conferred upon them by their respective charters, without looking beyond the seal or the royal parchment for the measure of their rights and the rule of their duties. The founders of Plymouth had been impelled by the peculiarities of their situation to examine the subject with deeper and more comprehensive research.* The thoughts derived from the Mayflower Compact can still be viewed in the governing documents of America today.

Plymouth Rock

Plymouth Rock is located in Plymouth, Massachusetts weighing today about ten tons. The Pilgrims decided on this landing site because much of the land was already cleared, a *sweet brooke ran under the hill side,* and *in this brooke* there was *much good fish in their seasons.* The Pilgrims decided that *we may harbour our Shallops and Boates exceeding well* in this place, and there was a great hill on which to *plant our Ordinance which will command all round about, from thence we may see into the Bay, and farre into the Sea, and we may see thence Cape Cod. (Mourt's Relation,* 1622, London)

Governor Bradford relates the landing on Plymouth Rock in his *Plimoth Plantation 1620-1647* as follows:

Chapter X

...On Monday they sounded ye harbor, and founde it fitt for shipping; and marched into ye land, & found diverse cornfeilds, & litl runing brooks, a place (as they supposed) fitt for situation; at least it was ye best they could find, and ye season, & their presente necessitie, made them glad to accepte of it. So they returned to their shipp againe with this news to ye rest of their people, which did much comforte their harts.

On ye 15. of Desem(r): they wayed anchor to goe to ye place they had discovered, & came within 2. leagues of it, but were faine to bear up againe; but ye 16. day ye winde came faire, and they arrived safe in this harbor. And after wards tooke better view of ye place, and resolved wher to pitch their dwelling; and ye 25. day begane to erecte ye first house for comone use to receive them and their goods.

The first steps of the Pilgrims onto Plymouth Rock from their shallop after deciding on the place of settlement must have brought about a whole myriad of emotions. First they were relieved to disembark from over a three-month stay on the *Mayflower*. Second the exhilaration of a new home on a new continent probably conveyed hope though tinged with fear of the unknown, but the joy of being able to worship the LORD as found in the Holy Bible must have reassured their hearts of a mission well chosen. Their choice of a new home had been decided, and there was no turning back. This is where they would rear their children, build their homes, and sooner than they realized; bury their family members and their friends. The foundation had been laid, and they were ready to build.

...the Mayflower sailed across the bay and dropped anchor in the inner harbor. And here began the settlement of the town consecrated to the idea of free and independent thought and worship and of just government and that may well be termed the nucleus of what has since so wonderfully developed into this grand and beloved country, of which we are justly proud. (Pilgrim Plymouth Guide, 1921 by W.F. Atwood, p. 14)

Much has been questioned concerning Plymouth Rock and the landing of the Pilgrims at that location, but testimonies from as far back as the original Pilgrims help confirm the facts. Mr. W. F. Atwood, from the line of Governor William Bradford, shares an account of the authentication of Plymouth Rock.

Plymouth Rock...has been viewed by many thousands of people, not only from our states, but all over the world. It has been photographed, painted and reproduced in bronze. Hereon the Pilgrims first stepped December 21, 1620. To those who may be prone to skepticism it may be stated that its interesting history has been handed down from generation to generation from Elder Thomas Faunce, who was born in Plymouth in 1647, and who died in 1746, aged 99 years. A few years before his death at a time when removal or covering up of the Rock was under contemplation, he made vigorous protest at what he termed the desecration of deep veneration, stating that his father, John Faunce, who came over in the Ann in 1623, had told him that it was on the Rock that the forefathers landed as stated by them to him.

It is further possible that at an early age some of the eldest of the <u>Mayflower</u> passengers may have reported this information to him directly. During the War of the Revolution, an attempt was made to remove the Rock to Town Square, there to be viewed as an emblem of liberty, civic and religious. In the operation of lifting, the upper portion split away leaving the base on its original bed. This top portion was, however, transferred to the square, where it remained until 1834, when it was taken to Pilgrim Hall and placed within an iron fence at the left of the entrance. In 1880 it was moved back and cemented on to its original base. (Pilgrim Plymouth Guide by W. F. Atwood, 1921, p. 40)

Burial Sites of the Pilgrim Fathers

For America, the sacred grounds of Arlington National Cemetery speak of lives sacrificed for a well-chosen mission; ensuring freedom lives on for America's future generations. This should never be forgotten. These honored dead knew the importance of strengthening the foundation which had been laid in the year 1620 by the Pilgrim Fathers. Let us go to Plymouth, Massachusetts and view the humble, resting places of the Pilgrim Fathers who came over on the *Mayflower* so many years ago in the birthing of the United States of America. These were buried as a corn of wheat whose seed blossomed into a bountiful harvest of stories; stories of sacrifice, toil, and victories won in the foundational days of America.

Three burial places are Cole's Hill and Burial Hill in Plymouth, and Myles Standish's Burying Ground in Duxbury. In the founding days of the Plymouth colony the shoreline was divided into acreage for farms, and soon expanded into two more colonies; Duxbury, first known as Duxborough, and Marshfield. These three colonies are close in proximity and became the founding colonies of the Pilgrim Fathers.

View of Cole's Hill in the Late 1800s with the Plymouth Rock Canopy to the Left

Cole's Hill was the burial place used for those Pilgrims who died the first winter. The Hill is named after an innkeeper named James Cole and his brother, John Cole, who was the owner of the property. Mr. W.F. Atwood stated in his book on page 42, *This spot is the resting place of those who succumbed the first fateful winter. The hardship of the voyage and the lack of proper accommodations after landing, developed much sickness and disease which made frightful inroads on the colony, their numbers being reduced by one-half during the period of a few months, those remaining being "scarce able to bury the dead." They were reduced so fast and to such an extent that it was deemed wise to conceal the graves, so they planted corn thereupon, that the Indians might remain in ignorance of their great losses.* With the passing of years, there were several times excavations and even water-main work revealed remains of those buried on Cole's Hill in unmarked graves. Some were re-interred while others were moved to Burial Hill.

In a storm of 1735 a torrent pouring down Middle Street made a ravine in Cole's Hill and washed many human remains down into the harbor...In 1855... graves were exposed in laying the public conduit on Cole's Hill. In one grave lay two skeletons, pronounced by surgeons male and female. The man had a particularly noble forehead; and it was fondly surmised that here were the remains of Mr. and Mrs. Carver. (The first governor of Plymouth and his wife who both died the first year, 1621) *These found a new grave on Burial Hill...all found* (on Cole's Hill were) *buried with their feet to the east.* (Here also is where Captain Myles Standish buried his first wife, Rose.) (*The Pilgrim Republic 1879* by John A. Goodwin, 1920 edition, p. 158)

Site of the First Fort

Burial Hill was the original site of the Pilgrims' first fort and meeting house built in 1621. As you stroll through town on Leyden Street in Plymouth, you will come to several churches in Town Square behind which rises Burial Hill. As you ascend the base of the hill, you are moved by the old, head stones covering the sacred hill. Walking up the steps, you begin to realize you are entering the solitude of Pilgrim graves each having a story to tell. Standing at the top of Burial Hill facing east, you are looking directly at Plymouth Bay and Plymouth Rock with the fort on your right and a memorial stone on your left marking the grave of Governor William Bradford.

Burial Hill, Plymouth

William Bradford's Memorial

One inscription on Governor Bradford's memorial is in Hebrew and when translated states, *Let the right hand of the Lord awake.* On a beautiful day not only is the view breathtaking, but thought-provoking as you remember the sacrifice these brave men and women faced as they willingly laid the foundation for America in the year 1620. *...England at that date had neither colony nor permanent settlement on the American coast. Emigration was then, in fact, expulsion beyond the limits of civilization, and involved not only danger and suffering to all, but inevitable death to a large proportion of the settlers. This was so much the case, that, up to the time of the exile of the Pilgrim Fathers, no American colony had succeeded, though many had been attempted...*(The Illustrated Pilgrim Memorial, Pilgrim Society, 1872, p. 23) Others interred on Burial Hill are John Howland who was the last of the *Mayflower* passengers who lived in Plymouth, Mary and Thomas Cushman, General James Warren, Thomas Faunce, William Crowe, John Cotton, and dependents of Governor William Bradford.

Grave of John Howland

Grave of William Crowe

The Miles Standish Monument, Duxbury

Just a short distance from Plymouth you will come to the town of Duxbury which is the location of Captain Myles Standish's Burial Ground. Myles Standish was an English, military officer enlisted by the Pilgrims who played a large role in advising and protecting the Plymouth Colony. This burial site is said to be the location of Duxbury's first meeting house and the resting place of several of the *Mayflower* passengers of 1620; Myles Standish, John and Priscilla Alden, and George Soule. This cemetery was left in disrepair for many years and after two exhumations in the 1800s has become one of the oldest, managed cemeteries in the United States.

National Monument to the Forefathers

Less than a mile away from Burial Hill stands a monument revealing the road map to Liberty called the *National Monument to the Forefathers* which was built by the Pilgrim Society who laid its cornerstone on August 1, 1859. It was finally completed and dedicated August 1, 1889 some 269 years after the Pilgrims first stepped on to Plymouth Rock. This monument

NATIONAL MONUMENT TO THE FOREFATHERS

was designed by Hammatt Billings, a distinguished artist and architect from Boston, Massachusetts. The citizens of that day did not want America to lose sight of her foundation so carefully laid by her Pilgrim Fathers. This foundation is distinctly portrayed in every part of this monument. As you view the pictures of the monument's beginning, you will notice there are no trees around the monument. It has been said that at this time it could be viewed from all around the Plymouth region, whether by land or sea, because it was set on one of the highest elevations in the area, but today it is hidden from the public's eye by development as well as tall trees. Some writers note that people living in the region do not even know the monument exists. America, it is time to reclaim a fading part of history which proclaims a vital prescription for the preservation of liberty.

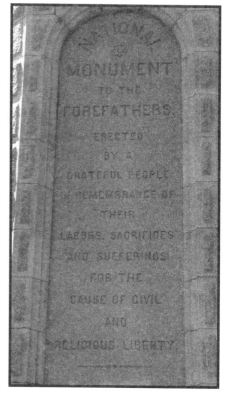

The Dedication Panel of the monument reads as follows:

NATIONAL MONUMENT TO THE FOREFATHERS ERECTED BY A GRATEFUL PEOPLE IN REMEMBRANCE OF THEIR LABORS, SACRIFICES, AND SUFFERINGS FOR THE CAUSE OF CIVIL AND RELIGIOUS LIBERTY.

The National Park Service Plaque reads:

THE NATIONAL MONUMENT TO THE FOREFATHERS WAS ADDED TO THE NATIONAL REGISTER OF HISTORIC PLACES BY THE NATIONAL PARK SERVICE, THE DEPARTMENT OF INTERIOR IN SEPTEMBER 1974. THE MONUMENT, DESIGNED BY HAMMATT BILLINGS OF BOSTON, WAS ERECTED BY THE PILGRIM SOCIETY IN 1889. IT POSSESSES EXCEPTIONAL VALUE IN COMMEMORATING AND ILLUSTRATING THE HISTORY OF THE UNITED STATES.

The monument taking thirty years to complete is made of Maine granite; standing 81 feet tall, weighing 180 tons, and costing $150,000 in the 1800s. It is greatly respected by those who have seen it. The first time my wife and I saw it, we were amazed by its seclusion. As we arrived at the site we saw one other vehicle and a family being guided around the monument. As we approached the monument we did not understand the foundational truths portrayed on it, but soon found ourselves circling the monument several times to take in the message revealed. Like in our circumstance, this granite monument will guide you to understand how true liberty is attained.

Lady Faith

The tallest figure is Lady Faith who is founded on four major standards of liberty personified by four figures named **Morality, Law, Education, and Liberty** who are each sitting at the feet of Faith. This depicts morality, law, education, and liberty are all seated in faith. Each seated figure is in itself revealing a truth which is reinforced by two virtues on either side of the seated figure as well as an additional carving of activities of the Pilgrim Fathers.

Lady Faith with a star on her forehead is pointing toward heaven holding an opened Bible in her left hand while standing on a pedestal; her left foot resting on Plymouth Rock. Lady Faith reveals America's liberty comes through the knowledge of God found in the Holy Bible lifted up in one's life by applying Its truths to one's heart and one's daily living. As one reads the Holy Bible, which is God's Word from heaven, that one who reads can be changed by faith in those words setting the heart at liberty. Lady Faith, the very beginning of liberty, found a foothold in America on Plymouth Rock desiring to share her knowledge of God with those in the New World.

Pilgrims' Embarkation

Prophet

Morality

Evangelist

Morality is an internal faith that comes through an internal regeneration. An individual reads God's Word, believes in Christ's redeeming salvation, and that one is changed. Morality is on her chair holding in her left hand the Ten Commandment and in her right hand a scroll of the book of Revelation. On the sides of her chair a **Prophet** is proclaiming truth while an **Evangelist** is sharing the good news of salvation. The carving below in front of Morality is the **Pilgrims' Embarkation** representing the willingness of the Pilgrim Fathers to share the Gospel in America.

Indian Treaty Carving

Mercy

Law

Justice

Law is the next standard seated in faith. Faith in God brings an adherence to God's laws as well as civic laws. Law is holding civil law in his left hand and extending his right hand in mercy. On one side of Law's chair is **Justice** depicted by scales, and on the other side is **Mercy**. The carving below in front of Law is the **Pilgrims' Treaty with the Indians**.

Pilgrims' Mayflower Compact

Wisdom

Education

Youth

Education sits in faith wearing a wreath of victory and pointing to the Bible. America must train her children in God's truth. On one side of Education's chair is **Youth** revealed by a mother educating her child, and on the other side is **Wisdom** rendered by a grandfather gesturing to the Bible and the Ten Commandments. A globe portrays that the Word of God will give a proper worldview. The carving below in front of Education is the signing of the **Pilgrims' Mayflower Compact** emphasizing the importance of civic education in light of God's Word.

Tyranny

Liberty

Peace

Liberty rests in faith holding a broken chain with shackles in his left hand and cradling a sword with his right arm. He is sitting on the skin of a defeated lion with its paw resting on his shoulder and the lion's head protruding from his back right. Liberty pictures the freedom from England the Pilgrims attained and the knowledge that this freedom must be protected or be lost. On one side of Liberty's chair is **Tyranny** exposing the Victor with his hand up in the air and his foot on the chest of the defeated, tyrant King. On the other side of Liberty's chair is its by-product, **Peace**. The carving below Liberty is the **Pilgrims' Landing at Plymouth Rock**.

Landing at Plymouth Rock

THUS OUT OF SMALL
BEGINNINGS GREATER THINGS
HAVE BEEN PRODUCED BY HIS
HAND THAT MADE ALL THINGS
OF NOTHING AND GIVES BEING
TO ALL THINGS THAT ARE;
AND AS ONE SMALL CANDLE
MAY LIGHT A THOUSAND, SO
THE LIGHT HERE KINDLED
HATH SHONE UNTO MANY, YEA
IN SOME SORT TO OUR WHOLE
NATION: LET THE GLORIOUS
NAME OF JEHOVAH HAVE ALL
THE PRAISE.
GOVERNOR WILLIAM BRADFORD

William Bradford Quote

The monument also shares a quote from Governor William Bradford:

THUS OUT OF SMALL BEGINNINGS GREATER THINGS HAVE BEEN PRODUCED BY HIS HAND THAT MADE ALL THINGS OF NOTHING AND GIVES BEING TO ALL THINGS THAT ARE; AND AS ONE SMALL CANDLE MAY LIGHT A THOUSAND, SO THE LIGHT HERE KINDLED HATH SHONE UNTO MANY, YEA IN SOME SORT TO OUR WHOLE NATION; LET THE GLORIOUS NAME OF JEHOVAH HAVE ALL PRAISE.

We may conclude from this great monument that faith plays a major part in the life of a nation. **FAITH** in the Holy Bible which is God's Word will bring **MORALITY**, will bring obedience to the **LAW**, will bring a great source for our children's **EDUCATION**, and **FAITH** will bring the breaking of the chains of tyranny to a nation and will give her citizens **LIBERTY** and peace. By faith all of these standards and virtues may be attained in the United States of America. This monument was built with future generations in mind. There is a large, empty space below Governor Bradford's quote which is available for etching. I wonder what will be engraved in this portion of smooth, Maine granite?

Conclusion

We have seen, then, several of the first foundations that were laid particularly by the determined Pilgrim Fathers of Plymouth Colony; their Mayflower Compact, their first steps onto Plymouth Rock, their burial sites, and the *National Monument to the Forefathers.* Governor William Bradford understood the importance of their mission that emotional morning in the year 1620 when leaving the port of Leyden, Holland for the shores of the New World. As Plymouth was in its infancy, Governor Bradford states in his *Of Plimoth Plantation 1620-1647* in chapter four:

*Lastly, (and which was not least,) a great hope & inward zeall they had of laying some **good foundation**, or at least to make some way thereunto, for ye propagating & advancing ye gospell of ye kingdom of Christ in those remote parts of ye world; yea, though they should be but even as stepping-stones unto others for ye performing of so great a work.*

Chapter Three

Foundations of the Family

Home; the word itself stirs emotions. The homes comprising America in its early beginning bear reflection if one is to understand the foundations upon which they were built. Parent and child of one generation to the next of youthful America seem to have fine-woven threads which tie them all together making a beautiful tapestry. For sake of space, we have researched the homes of only two great Americans; President George Washington and President Abraham Lincoln. The parents and children of these homes chose foundational principles which still strengthen families in America today. What did these two great families have in common?

James A. Garfield

James A. Garfield, the twentieth President of the United States, felt the profound influence of Abraham Lincoln. Garfield's personal childhood echoed some of the hardships Lincoln endured and overcame. Garfield also was born in the wilderness but in Ohio instead of Kentucky, living in a log cabin, losing one of his parents when he was a child, and working manual labor on the farm to help provide for the family. Faith in God and the Bible helped them persevere. Garfield had his eyes on the life of President Lincoln almost 20 years prior to his own election in 1881.

AN AMERICAN FARMSTEAD.

Picture from the Story of Garfield by William G. Rutherford 1895

Columbus, February 16, 1861

Garfield to B.A. Hinsdale.

Mr. Lincoln...On the whole, I am greatly pleased with him. He clearly shows his want of culture, and the marks of Western life; but there is no touch of affectation in him, and he has a peculiar power of impressing you that he is frank, direct, and thoroughly honest. His remarkable good sense, simple and condensed style of expression, and evident marks of indomitable will, give me great hopes for the country.

(The Life of Gen. James A. Garfield, J.M. Bundy, New York: A.S. Barnes & Co., 1880, p. 51)

President Abraham Lincoln

Abraham Lincoln's parents were born in Virginia of "undistinguished" families as President Lincoln called them. His paternal grandfather was also named Abraham Lincoln. His father, Thomas, in 1806 married his mother, Nancy Hanks. President Lincoln wrote in his family Bible the birthdates of his parents along with the date of their marriage. He said of his mother that she was "highly intellectual by nature, had a strong memory, acute judgment

Abraham Lincoln

and was cool and heroic." Many Hanks in early America were men who prayed, preached from the King James Bible, and exhorted men unto salvation. Nancy Hanks' father was also named Abraham. This was the same Abraham Hanks who was a Revolutionary War veteran, and who came to Kentucky with the Boones being a great friend to Daniel Boone as stated by his grandson, William Hanks. Both of Nancy's parents died when she was a child leaving her an orphan. She was "farmed out" to the Shipley family and then to the Berry family. Being married in Kentucky, Thomas and Nancy were blessed with a daughter, Sarah, and then a son, Abraham who was born on February 8, 1809. He was named after his mother's father. Another son was born, but he died in infancy.

The following excerpts from Thayer's book are included especially since President Lincoln provided, at Thayer's request, names and addresses of Lincoln's friends and acquaintances who could best assist Thayer in offering information for this book. When the book was published, Thayer presented a copy to President Lincoln.

55

The Pioneer Boy

and

How He Became President

By William M. Thayer
Boston: Walker, Wise, and Company
245 Washington Street
1864

pp. 20-21
(Hardin County, Kentucky)

...they lived in a log-house...a dwelling without a floor, furnished with four or five three-legged stools, pots, kettles, spider Dutch-oven, and something that answered for a bed. The man's name was Thomas Lincoln, and both he and his wife were members of the Baptist Church, in good standing. Mrs. Lincoln, particularly, was a whole-hearted Christian, and the influence of her godly example and precepts was felt by each member of the family. She was a woman of marked natural abilities, but of little culture. She could read, but was not able to write. Her good judgment and sound common sense, united with her strong mental powers and deep-toned piety, made her a remarkable woman.

THE OLD LINCOLN CABIN

Mr. Lincoln was not so highly endowed by nature, yet he was superior to most of his neighbors in all the attributes of respectable manhood. He was of rather a practical turn of mind, and a somewhat close observer of men and things. He could neither read nor write, with this exception, that he could write his name so that some people could read it. His father before him was poor, and, what was worse, he was killed by the Indians when Thomas was a boy, so that the latter was sent adrift to shift for himself. Hard times and harder fortune oppressed him everywhere that he went, and he had all he could do to earn enough to keep soul and body together, without going to school a single day. He realized his deficiencies, and thought all the more of learning, because he was deprived of it himself. He was a kind, industrious, practical, pious man, and his determination and perseverance enabled him to accomplish whatever he undertook.

p. 22
...Abraham was seven years old when he was sent to school, for the first time, (to Riney and then) *to one Hazel, who came to live in the neighborhood. There were no schools nor school-houses in the region, and few of the people around could read. But this Hazel could read and write; but beyond this he made a poor figure. For a small sum he taught a few children at his house, and Abraham was one of the number. His parents were so anxious that he should know how to read and write, that they managed to save enough out of their penury to send him to school a few weeks. They considered Abraham a remarkable boy...*

p. 45
...Abraham went on with his school. Every day he posted away with the old spelling-book to Hazel's cabin, where he tried as hard to learn as any boy who ever studied his Ab's. He carried his book home at night, and puzzled his active brain over what he had learned during the day. He cared for nothing but his book now. His highest ambition was to learn to read as well as his mother could. As she gathered the family around her, and read the Bible to them each day...he almost envied her the blessed privilege of reading. He longed for the day to come when he could read aloud from that revered volume.

p. 53
...(His mother's) reading was not confined to the Old Testament, nor to the narrative portions of the Bible. She understood the Gospel because she had a Christian experience that was marked. She was a firm, consistent disciple of the Lord Jesus, and was qualified thereby to expound the Scriptures. The story of the Cross, as it is recorded in the twenty-seventh chapter of Matthew, was read over and over at the fireside, accompanied with many remarks that were suited to impress the minds of her children.

"Yes, you ought to love him and serve him," she would say, "for all his love and mercy. He died for you, and he has a claim on your hearts."

p. 58
...She was very familiar with the Bible, and its authority was always appealed to as above on the sin of lying.

"No; my children must never lie. Better be poor than be false. There is nothing worse than lying."

...It was the first book that Abraham ever read,--that same old family Bible, kept very choice because their poverty could not afford another. It was the only Bible that his mother ever possessed, her life-treasure, to which she was more indebted, and perhaps, also, her son Abraham, that to any other influence...

pp. 60-61
...A Christian mother's culture always makes its mark. Great and good men usually have good mothers. Their fathers may not be men of mark, but their mothers are women of noble powers and qualities of heart...

John Quincy Adams was another American statesman who bore similar testimony to the value of his mother's influence. "It is due to gratitude and nature," he said, "that I should acknowledge and avow that, such as I have been, whatever it was, such as I am, whatever it is, and such as I hope to be in all futurity, must be ascribed, under Providence, to the precepts and example of my mother."

(When Abe was eight, his family moved to Spencer County, Indiana to an unbroken forest. He was big for his age, so his father put an axe to his hand, and Abe helped clear the woods and continued using this useful instrument up until he was twenty-three.)

(Lincoln recalled he was age ten when his mother died.)

(After his mother died, Abe was kicked by a horse and almost died.)

pp. 124-125
...It was a great change that death wrought in the Lincoln family, and no one felt it more than Abraham. For some weeks his mind was absorbed in his loss. Not even his accustomed habits of study could avail to divert his thoughts from his great sorrow. His father took notice of it, and longed to afford him relief. At length he met with a copy of the "Pilgrim's Progress," at the house of an acquaintance, nearly twenty miles distant; and thinking that it would be a rich

treat to Abraham, and serve to cheer his lonely hours, he obtained the loan of the book. Carefully wrapping the volume, he conveyed it home.

...And it turned out to be so. Abraham sat down to read this volume very much as some other boys would sit down to a good dinner. He found it better even than he expected...

p. 133
(When Abe was about eleven he desired to read the life of George Washington.)

..."I want to read the life of George Washington." His grandfather lived when Washington was leading the American army to victory, and Abraham had heard many stories told by his father of those perilous times, and Washington was always the hero of the day. It was not surprising, then, that he had a strong desire to read the book.

(The reading of this book greatly influenced young Abe.)

p. 155
(Mr. Lincoln then married a Sally Johnston, a widow with three children. She was good and kind.)

...Boys are apt to take advantage of such circumstances, and claim greater liberties with step-mothers...But it was not so with Abraham. He received her as a mother, and loved and obeyed her as such. He was not more respectful to his own mother than he was to her...

(When twenty-three, Abe and his new family moved to Illinois where he helped split enough wood for a log cabin and enough rails for ten-acres of land.)

p. 172
...In all, he (Abraham) *did not go to school more than six months in his life...*

(Lincoln himself summed up the time to be about a year total.)

pp. 306-307

...That the foundation of his success was laid in his boyhood cannot be denied. We have seen that his early life was distinguished for those elements of character that have rendered his manhood conspicuous. An excellent mother's training appears in the beginning. Never was maternal influence more clearly illustrated in the rearing of a son. The three lessons that the mother of Washington said she endeavored to impress upon the mind of her son—namely, "obedience, diligence, and truth"—were insisted upon in his (Abe's) childhood. Never did a boy give more earnest heed to these cardinal virtues than did he. All along through his early life they appear,--the flower and fruit of a sainted mother's fidelity.

There was also an energy, perseverance, and decision manifest in all his acts... These qualities appear even in the sports of his boyhood. They characterize his early labors and studies.

...In this way his mental powers were developed with his physical. The mind and the body strengthened together. Small advantages produced great results.

Lincoln Studying

Self-control was an important characteristic of his early life. He did not use profane language when other boys did. He would forego the pleasures of companionship to assist his parents. He could sacrifice a good time in frolic for the enjoyment of reading a book. Though living when almost every one used intoxicating drinks, he kept his appetite in subjection, and practiced remarkable abstinence. Says one who was a companion with him from ten to twenty-two years of age, "He was remarkably temperate...I never saw him take the smallest dram."

p. 309

...The labors and hardships of his early life, too, were just adapted to develop his physical nature into remarkable powers of endurance, as if a wise Providence was preparing him for the responsibilities of the present hour, under which ordinary constitutions would fail...

Abraham Lincoln to Jesse W. Fell
Tuesday, December 20, 1859

My dear Sir:

Herewith is a little sketch as you requested—There is not much of it, for the reason, I suppose, that there is not much of me—If anything is made out of it, I wish it to be modest...

...when I came of age I did not know much—Still somehow, I could read, write, and cipher to the rule of Three, but that was all—I have not been to school since— The little advance I now have upon this store of education, I have picked up from time to time under the pressure of necessity—I was raised to farm work, which I continued till I was twenty-two—

James Q. Howard, Biographical Notes
May 1860

His pants were made of flax and tow...his knees were both out. Was the roughest looking man I ever saw—poor boy, but welcomed to everybody's house.

Henry McHenry – A good friend of Lincoln

When he used to speak there was always profound silence—Never knew him to swear or drink a drop of liquor in his life."

Hon. John T. Stuart's Statement

About this time (1832) he got some mathematical works and a Surveyor's compass and made his living by surveying.

L.M. Green – A lawyer of Petersburgh

I never knew him in one instance to deviate from the strictest principles of integrity and morality.

Dennis Hanks – Cousin to Lincoln (ten years older than Lincoln)

He was a very good boy and an earnest man so was his father before him. His mother belonged to the Baptist Church, a Christian lady in every respect.

Cornelia Fonda to Abraham Lincoln
Thursday, January 28, 1864

...you sir, had so good and godly a mother, possessing stern virtues and strength of character with powers of so much endurance and that she loved the Bible that by it and prayer all her life was so imbued...

Benjamin Talbot to Abraham Lincoln
December 21, 1864
Iowa City, Iowa,

Dear Sir,

I cannot refrain from expressing to you my joy, (& I doubt not the joy of every Christian heart throughout our land), at the statement made in the religious press that you have sought & found the Savior, that you "do love Jesus"...

Salmon P. Chase to Mary Todd Lincoln
Saturday, March 01, 1865
Washington

Dear Madam,

Will you oblige me by accepting the Bible, kissed by your honored husband, on taking today, for the second time the oath of office as President of the United States..."

The Sun, New York
Thursday, September 8, 1864
PRICE: ONE CENT IN GOLD, TWO CENTS IN CURRENCY
(President Lincoln was presented a beautiful Bible from a committee in Baltimore in gratitude for his dedication to freedom for all. President Lincoln then responded to them.)

The President replied...In regard to the great book, I have only to say, it is the best gift which God has ever given man. All the good from the Savior of the world is communicated to us through this Book. But for that Book we could not know right from wrong. All those things desirable to man are contained in it. I return you my sincere thanks for this very elegant copy of this great Book of God, which you present.

We have thus far, then, seen the thread which entwined President Garfield's life to President Lincoln's life, and which now interlaces with the life of President George Washington. As stated in Thayer's biography, Abraham Lincoln was profoundly influenced by hearing his father's stories of President Washington and by reading the life of George Washington himself when he was about eleven. Abraham Lincoln wanted to know what made George Washington great because President Washington seemed to be everyone's hero in early America.

Lincoln Taking the Oath at His Second Inauguration
March 4, 1865

President George Washington

We begin with a quote from the last will and testament of George Washington's grandfather, Lawrence Washington, March 11, 1698, spelling not edited. (*The George Washington Papers* at the Library of Congress, 1741-1799)

IN THE NAME OF GOD AMEN I Lawrence Washington of Washington parish in the County of Westmo[re]land in Virginia gentleman being of good and perfect memory thanks be unto almighty God for it...this to be taken only for my Last will and Testament and no other. and first being heartily sorry from the bottom of my heart for my Sines most humbly deserving forgiveness of the same from the allmighty God my savior and Redeemer in whom by the merits of Jesus Christ I trust and beleive assuredly to be saved and to have full remission and forgiveness of all my Sines, and that my—Soule with my body at the general day of resurrection shall rise againe with joy and through the merits of Christs death and passion posses and inherit the Kingdom of heaven prepared for his Elect and chosen...

Mount Vernon

Recollections and Private Memoirs of Washington
By His Adopted Son, George Washington Parke Custis

With a Memoir of the Author
By His Daughter
And Explanatory Notes
By Benson J. Lossing

New York: Derby & Jackson
1860

The Mother of Washington
Mary Ball Washington

(Mary Ball Washington's father died when she was three years of age, and nine years later she became an orphan when her mother died. She went to live with her half-sister, Elizabeth. She married Augustine Washington on March 6, 1731 when she was twenty-two. Next to Jeremiah, chapter twenty-six in their leather-bound, family Bible now housed at Mt. Vernon is a page carefully inscribed with the marriage of Augustine Washington (ca. 1694-1743) and his second wife, Mary Ball (1708-1789), as well as the birth dates of their six children. *George Washington, son to Augustine & Mary his wife was born...about 10 in the morning...* on February 11, 1731/32, according to the Julian calendar then in use. In 1752 England adopted the Gregorian calendar which changed the date of George Washington's birthday to February 22, 1732. In 1743, after twelve years of marriage, Augustine passed away leaving Mary a widow. She never remarried.)

p. 129
(George's father) *died about middle age, universally esteemed as a man of worth and honor...He is described as having been of fair complexion, tall stature, and manly proportions. At the time of his father's death, George Washington was between eleven and twelve years of age. He has been heard to say, that he knew little of his father, other than a remembrance of his person, and of his parental fondness. Of the mother, that distinguished woman, to whose peculiar cast of character, and more than ancient discipline in the education of her illustrious son, himself ascribed the origin of his fortunes and his fame, we have much to say.*

(George Washington wrote of his mother in his papers on February 14, 1784 to the citizens of Fredericksburg, *"...the honorable mention wch. is made of my revered Mother; by whose maternal hand (early deprived of a Father) I was led from childhood.")*

Washington and His Mother

She was descended from the very respectable family of Ball, who settled as English colonists, on the banks of the Potomac (Her family coming from England settled in Lancaster County, Virginia around 1650.)

pp. 130-131

...The mother of Washington, in forming him for those distinguished parts he was destined to perform, first taught him the duties of obedience, the better to prepare him for those of command. In the well-ordered domicil, where his early years were passed, the levity and indulgence, common to youth, was tempered by a deference and well-regulated restraint, which, while it curtailed or suppressed no rational enjoyment, usual in the spring-time of life, prescribed those enjoyments within the bounds of moderation and propriety.

The matron held in reserve an authority, which never departed from her; not even when her son had become the most illustrious of men. It seemed to say, "I am your mother...the guide who directed your steps when they needed the guidance of age and wisdom, the parental affection which claimed your love, the parental authority which commanded your obedience; whatever may be your success, whatever your renown, next to your God you owe them most to me." Nor did the chief dissent from these truths, but to the last moments of the life of his venerable parent, he yielded to her will the most dutiful and implicit obedience, and felt for the person and character the most holy reverence and attachment.

This lady possessed not the ambition which is common to lesser minds; and the peculiar plainness, yet dignity of her habits and manners, became in nowise altered, when the sun of glory rose upon her house, in the character of her child. The late Lawrence Washington, Esq., of Chotank, one of the associates of the juvenile years of the chief, and remembered by him in his will, thus describes the home of the mother:---

"I was often there with George, his playmate, schoolmate, and young man's companion. Of the mother I was ten times more afraid than I ever was of my own parents. She awed me in the midst of her kindness, for she was, indeed, truly kind. I have often been present with her sons, proper tall fellows too, and we were all as mute as mice; and even now, when time has whitened my locks, and I am the grand-parent of a second generation, I could not behold that remarkable woman without feelings it is impossible to describe. Whoever has seen that awe-inspiring air and manner so characteristic in the Father of his Country, will remember the matron as she appeared when the presiding genius of her well-ordered household, commanding and being obeyed."

pp. 132-134
Of the many anecdotes touching the early life of the chief, we shall present our readers with one of no ordinary interest and character.

The blooded horse was the Virginian favorite of those days as well as these. Washington's mother, fond of the animal to which her deceased husband had been particularly attached, had preserved the race in its greatest purity, and at the time of our story possessed several young horses of superior promise.

One there was, a sorrel, destined to be as famous...This sorrel was of a fierce and ungovernable nature, and resisted all attempts to subject him to the rein. He had reached his fullest size and vigor, unconscious of a rider; he ranged free in the air, which he snuffed in triumph, tossing his mane to the winds, and spurning the earth in the pride of his freedom. It was a matter of common remark, that a man never would be found hardly enough to back and ride this vicious horse. Several had essayed, but deterred by the fury of the animal, they had desisted from their attempts, and the steed remained unbroken.

They young Washington proposed to his companions, that if they would assist him in confining the steed, so that a bridle could be placed in his mouth, he would engage to tame this terror of the parish. Accordingly, early the ensuing morning, the associates decoyed the horse into an inclosure, where they secured him, and the daring youth sprang to his unenvied seat, and bidding his comrades remove their tackle, the indignant courser rushed to the plain.

As if disdaining his burden, he at first attempted to fly, but soon felt the power of an arm which could have tamed his Arab grandsires, in their wildest course on their native deserts. The struggle now became terrific to the beholders, who almost wished that they had not joined in an enterprise, so likely to be fatal to their daring associate. But the youthful hero, that "spirit-protected man," clung to the furious steed, till centaur-like, he appeared to make part of the animal itself. Long was the conflict, and the fears of the associates became more relieved as, with matchless skill the rider preserved his seat, and with unyielding force controlled the courser's rage, when the gallant horse, summoning all his powers to one mighty effort, reared, and plunged with tremendous violence, burst his noble heart, and died in an instant.

The rider, "alive, unharmed, and without a wound," was joined by the youthful group, and all gazed upon the generous steed...

The first surprise was scarcely over...when the party were summoned to the morning's meal...the matron asking, "Pray, young gentlemen, have you seen my blooded colts in your rambles? I hope they are well taken care of; my favorite, I am told, is as large as his sire."

Considerable embarrassment being observable, the lady repeated her question, when George Washington replied, "Your favorite, the sorrel, is dead, madam."

"Dead," exclaimed the lady; "why, how has this happened?"

Nothing dismayed, the youth continued, "That sorrel horse has long been considered ungovernable, and beyond the power of man to back or ride him; this morning, aided by my friends, we forced a bit into his mouth; I backed him, I rode him, and in a desperate struggle for the mastery, he fell under me and died upon the spot."

The hectic of a moment was observed to flush on the matron's cheek, but like a summer cloud, it soon passed away, and all was serene and tranquil, when she remarked: "It is well; but while I regret the loss of my favorite, I rejoice in my son, who always speaks the truth."

At the time of this occurrence, the figure of the lad is described by his contemporaries as being that of the athlete of the games... manners somewhat grave and reserved... He particularly excelled in all the manly exercises, sought the companionship of the intelligent and deserving, and was beloved and admired by all who knew him.

...

When the comforting and glorious intelligence arrived of the passage of the Delaware (Dec. '76), an event which restored our hopes from the very brink of despair, a number of her friends waited upon the mother with congratulations. She received them with calmness... "but, my good sirs, here is too much flattery; still George will not forget the lessons I early taught him—he will not forget himself, though he is the subject of so much praise."

...

Always pious, in her latter days her devotions were performed in private. She was in the habit of repairing every day to a secluded spot, formed by rocks and trees near to her dwelling, where, abstracted from the world and worldly things, she communed with her Creator in humiliation and prayer. (This "Prayer Rock"

as she called it was close to her daughter's mansion on the Kenmore Plantation in Fredericksburg, Virginia. She asked her daughter, Betty, to bury her by her favorite "high-perched rock" in the garden. This request was granted and arranged by Betty.)

71

Mary Ball Washington's Prayer Rock

Immediately after the organization of the present government, the chief magistrate repaired to Fredericksburg, to pay his humble duty to his mother, preparatory to his departure for New York. An affecting scene ensued. The son feelingly remarked the ravages which a torturing disease had made upon the aged frame of the mother, and addressed her with these words: "The people, madam, have been pleased, with the most flattering unanimity, to elect me to the chief magistracy of these United States, but before I can assume the functions of my office, I have come to bid you an affectionate farewell. So soon as the weight of public business, which must necessarily attend the outset of a new government, can be disposed of, I shall hasten to Virginia, and"—Here the matron interrupted with—"and you will see me no more; my great age, and the disease which is fast approaching my vitals, warn me that I shall not be long in this world;...But go, George, fulfil the high destinies which Heaven appears to have intended you for; go, my son, and may that heaven's and a mother's blessing be with you always."

The president was deeply affected. His head rested upon the shoulder of his parent, whose aged arm feebly, yet fondly encircled his neck. That brow on which fame had wreathed the purest laurel virtue ever gave to created man, relaxed from its *lofty bearing. That look which could have awed a Roman senate in its Fabrician day, was bent in filial tenderness upon the time-worn features of the aged matron. He wept. A thousand recollections crowded upon his mind, as memory retracing scenes long passed, carried him back to the maternal mansion and the days of juvenility, where he beheld that mother, whose care, education, and discipline, caused him to reach the topmost height of laudable ambition. Yet, how were his glories forgotten, while he gazed upon her whom, wasted by time and malady, he should part with...Her predictions were but too true. The disease which so long had preyed upon her frame, completed its triumph, and she expired at the age of eighty-five, rejoicing in the consciousness of a life well spent, and confiding in the belief of a blessed immortality.*

...

In her latter days, the matron often spoke of her own good boy; of the merits of his early life; of his love and duty; but of the deliverer of his country—the chief magistrate of the great republic, never. Call you this insensibility? Call you it want of ambition? Oh, no; her ambition had been gratified to overflowing. In her Spartan school she had taught him to be good—that he became great, was a consequence, not the cause.

Tomb of Mary, Mother of Washington

The original monument (on left) as it appeared before the present granite obelisk (on right) was erected over the grave of George Washington's mother in Fredericksburg, Virginia.

The Farmer Boy and How He Became Commander-in-Chief

By Uncle Juvinell
Edited by William M. Thayer

Boston: Walker, Wise, and Company
245 Washington Street
1864

p. 37
...At the age of five...his parents started him to school...
His first teacher was a Mr. Hobby...

p. 40
...A more prudent and careful father, and a more discreet and affectionate mother, than Mr. Washington and his wife Mary, perhaps never lived. So earnest and watchful were they to bring up their children in the fear of the Lord, and in the practice of every noble virtue, that their dutiful behavior and sweet manners were the talk and praise of the good people for miles and miles around. They taught them to be neat and orderly in their dress, as well as civil and polite in their manners; to be respectful to their elders; to be kind to one another, and to every thing God hath made, both great and small, whether man or bird or beast: but chiefly were they concerned to teach them the love of truth, and to tell it at all times when it should be their duty to speak out, let the consequences be what they might.

p. 48
...(George Washington's father) by industry and prudent management, had gathered together enough of the riches of this world to leave each of his children a fine plantation...

...It has been often remarked, that those men who have most distinguished themselves in the world's history for noble thoughts and heroic deeds, have, as a general thing, inherited those qualities of mind and heart which made them great, from their mothers, rather than from their fathers; and also that their efforts to improve and elevate the condition of their fellow-beings have been owing in a larger measure to the lessons of truth, piety, and industry, taught them by their mothers in childhood and early youth...

Washington Parting with His Mother

Memoirs of the Mother and Wife of Washington

BY MARGARET C. CONKLING
AUBURN:
DERBY, MILLER, AND COMPANY.
1850

(George Washington's Mother)

pp. 21-22

Mrs. Washington had, henceforth, the exclusive direction of the primary education of her children. At once their companion, mentor, counsellor, and friend, she encouraged them to mental exertion, to moral culture, to athletic exercise...

p. 26

...Mrs. Washington was a CHRISTIAN MATRON, who derived her ideas of parental authority and government from the same BOOK (the Holy Bible) wherein she sought her own rules of life...

(She would read to her children from Sir Matthew Hale's *Contemplations Moral and Divine*, 1685. This is a collection of short devotions from the Holy Bible. This book found in George Washington's library after his death had Mary Ball's signature in it and had the appearance of frequent use with marks of reference. It was last known to be in a private collection in the late-nineteenth century. Another book belonging to George Washington was Offspring Blackall's 1717 *The Sufficiency of a Standing Revelation in General*. This book is believed to have been given to George by his parents because of his boyish signature appearing in it. It teaches that there is no need for further revelation since we have the final revelation from the LORD in the Old and New Testaments of the Holy Bible. Different religious groups during this time period were still seeking new revelation from God. It is now in the collection of the Boston Athenaeum.)

(Titles of books with their current locations; compliments of George Washington's Mount Vernon associate curator, Mount Vernon, Virginia)

p. 30
Chief Justice Marshall states, "Stimulated by the enthusiasm of military genius, to take part in the war in which Great Britain was then engaged, he (George) had pressed so earnestly to enter the navy, that, at the age of fifteen, a midshipman's warrant was obtained for him."

But the numerous biographers of Washington, however they may differ in other respects, agree in ascribing his abandonment of this cherished scheme to the all-powerful influence of his mother. One of them affirms that the luggage of the young enthusiast was actually conveyed on board the little vessel destined to bear him away to his new post, and that, when he attempted to bid adieu to his only parent, his previous resolution to depart was for the first time subdued, in consequence of her ill-concealed dejection and her irrepressible tears...

p. 47
And when, after the lapse of long, dark years of national gloom and suffering, Mrs. Washington was, at last, informed of the crowning event of the great conflict— the surrender of Lord Cornwallis, she raised her hands with profound reverence and gratitude towards heaven, and fervently exclaimed, "Thank God!—war will now be ended, and peace, independence and happiness bless our country!"

p. 70
...she sought to obtain from the Bible alone her invariable rule of life...

p. 72
*...Enshrined in the **Sanctuary of Home**, her sublime example is the peerless boast of her country...*

BIRTH-PLACE OF WASHINGTON.

Maxims Written in George Washington's Copy Book

Discipline and proper etiquette were important in the Washington home. To reinforce them, writing seemed to be a perfect solution. The date of 1745 was written in George's Copy Book making him about thirteen at the time of this writing exercise. These maxims formed his decorum throughout his teenage and adult life. The hand-written original has ripped corners making some of the maxims incomplete. They are filled in with corresponding maxims from the book, *Youths Behaviour*, or, *Decency in Conversation Amongst Men* translated from French into English by Francis Hawkins, 1668. The poem, *On Christmas Day*, was also written in his Copy Book. Because of a ripped corner, the missing words were taken from the poem, *On Christmas Day* by Orinthia, found in the *Gentleman's Magazine*, London, February 1743, p. 96. Any spelling or grammatical differences were kept as found in the hand-written original as young George copied them.

1. Every Action done in Company, ought to be with Some Sign of Respect, to those that are Present.
2. When in Company, put not your Hands to any Part of the Body, not usualy Discovered.
3. Shew Nothing to your Friend that may affright him.

78

4. In the Presence of Others Sing not to yourself with a humming Noise, nor Drum with your Fingers or Feet.

5. If You Cough, Sneeze, Sigh, or Yawn, do it not Loud but Privately; and speak not in your Yawning, but put Your handkerchief or Hand before your face and turn aside.

6. Sleep not when others Speak, Sit not when others stand, Speak not when you Should hold your Peace, walk not on when others Stop.

7. Put not off your Cloths in the presence of Others, nor go out your Chamber half Drest.

8. At Play and at Fire it's Good manners to Give Place to the last Commer, and affect not to Speak Louder than Ordinary.

9. Spit not in the Fire, nor Stoop low before it neither Put your Hands into the Flames to warm them, nor Set your Feet upon the Fire especially if there be meat before it.

10. When you Sit down, Keep your Feet firm and Even; without putting one on the other or Crossing them.

11. Shift not yourself in the Sight of others nor Gnaw your nails.

12. Shake not the head, Feet, or Legs rowl not the Eys lift not one eyebrow higher than the other wry not the mouth, and bedew no mans face with your Spittle, by appr[oaching too nea]r him [when] you Speak.

13. Kill no Vermin as Fleas, lice ticks &c in the Sight of Others, if you See any filth or thick Spittle put your foot Dexteriously upon it if it be upon the Cloths of your Companions, Put it off privately, and if it be upon your own cloths return Thanks to him who puts it off.

14. Turn not your Back to others especially in Speaking, Jog not the Table or Desk on which Another reads or writes, lean not upon any one.

15. Keep your Nails clean and Short, also your Hands and Teeth Clean yet without Shewing any great Concern for them.

16. Do not Puff up the Cheeks, Loll not out the tongue rub the Hands, or beard, thrust out the lips, or bite them or keep the Lips too open or too Close.

17. Be no Flatterer, neither Play with any that delights not to be Play'd Withal.

18. Read no Letters, Books, or Papers in Company but when there is a Necessity for the doing of it you must ask leave: come not near the Books or Writings of Another so as to read them unless desired or give your opinion of them unask'd also look not nigh when another is writing a Letter.

19. Let your Countenance be pleasant but in Serious Matters Somewhat grave.

20. The Gestures of the Body must be Suited to the discourse you are upon.

21. Reproach none for the Infirmaties of Nature, nor Delight to Put them that have in mind thereof.

22. Shew not yourself glad at the Misfortune of Another though he were your enemy.

23. When you see a Crime punished, you may be inwardly Pleased; but always shew Pity to the Suffering Offender.

24. [Do not laugh too loud or] too much at any Publick [Spectacle].

25. Superfluous Complements and all Affectation of Ceremonie are to be avoided, yet where due they are not to be Neglected.

26. In Pulling off your Hat to Persons of Distinction, as Noblemen, Justices, Churchmen &c make a Reverence, bowing more or less according to the Custom of the Better Bred, and Quality of the Person. Amongst your equals expect not always that they Should begin with you first, but to Pull off the Hat when there is no need is Affectation, in the Manner of Saluting and resaluting in words keep to the most usual Custom.

27. Tis ill manners to bid one more eminent than yourself be covered as well as not to do it to whom it's due Likewise he that makes too much haste to Put on his hat does not well, yet he ought to Put it on at the first, or at most the Second time of being ask'd; now what is herein Spoken, of Qualification in behavior in Saluting, ought also to be observed in taking of Place, and Sitting down for ceremonies without Bounds is troublesome.

28. If any one come to Speak to you while you are are Sitting Stand up tho he be your Inferiour, and when you Present Seats let it be to every one according to his Degree.

29. When you meet with one of Greater Quality than yourself, Stop, and retire especially if it be at a Door or any Straight place to give way for him to Pass.

30. In walking the highest Place in most Countrys Seems to be on the right hand therefore Place yourself on the left of him whom you desire to Honour; but if three walk together the mid[ ] Place is the most Honourable the wall is usually given to the most worthy if two walk together.

31. If any one far Surpasses others, either in age, Estate, or Merit [yet] would give Place to a meaner than hims[elf in his own lodging or elsewhere] the one ought not to except it, S[o he on the other part should not use much earnestness nor offer] it above once or twice.

32. To one that is your equal, or not much inferior you are to give the chief Place in your Lodging and he to who 'tis offered ought at the first to refuse it but at the Second to accept though not without acknowledging his own unworthiness.

33. They that are in Dignity or in office have in all places Preceedency but whilst they are Young they ought to respect those that are their equals in Birth or other Qualitys, though they have no Publick charge.

34. It is good Manners to prefer them to whom we Speak befo[re] ourselves especially if they be above us with whom in no Sort we ought to begin.

35. *Let your Discourse with Men of Business be Short and Comprehensive.*

36. *Artificers & Persons of low Degree ought not to use many ceremonies to Lords, or Others of high Degree but Respect and high[ly] Honour them, and those of high Degree ought to treat them with affability & Courtesie, without Arrogancy.*

37. *In Speaking to men of Quality do not lean nor Look them full in the Face, nor approach too near them at lest Keep a full Pace from them.*

38. *In visiting the Sick, do not Presently play the Physicion if you be not Knowing therein.*

39. *In writing or Speaking, give to every Person his due Title According to his Degree & the Custom of the Place.*

40. *Strive not with your Superiers in argument, but always Submit your Judgment to others with Modesty.*

41. *Undertake not to Teach your equal in the art himself Proffesses; it Savours of arrogancy.*

42. *[Let thy ceremonies in] Courtesie be proper to the Dignity of his place [with whom thou conversest for it is absurd to ac]t the same with a Clown and a Prince.*

43. *Do not express Joy before one sick or in pain for that contrary Passion will aggravate his Misery.*

44. *When a man does all he can though it Succeeds not well blame not him that did it.*

45. *Being to advise or reprehend any one, consider whether it ought to be in publick or in Private; presently, or at Some other time in what terms to do it & in reproving Shew no Sign of Cholar but do it with all Sweetness and Mildness.*

46. *Take all Admonitions thankfully in what Time or Place Soever given but afterwards not being culpable take a Time [&] Place convenient to let him know it that gave them.*

47. *Mock not nor Jest at any thing of Importance break [n]o Jest that are Sharp biting and if you Deliver any thing witty and Pleasant ab[s]tain from Laughing thereat yourself.*

48. *Wherein wherein you reprove Another be unblameable yourself; for example is more prevalent than Precepts.*

49. *Use no Reproachfull Language against any one neither Curse nor Revile.*

50. *Be not hasty to believe flying Reports to the Disparag[e]ment of any.*

51. *Wear not your Cloths, foul, unript or Dusty but See they be Brush'd once every day at least and take heed tha[t] you approach not to any Uncleaness.*

52. *In your Apparel be Modest and endeavor to accomodate Nature, rather than to procure Admiration keep to the Fashio[n] of your equals Such as are Civil and orderly with respect to Times and Places.*

53. Run not in the Streets, neither go t[oo s]lowly nor wit[h] Mouth open go not Shaking yr Arms [kick not the earth with yr feet, go] not upon the Toes, nor in a Dancing [fashion].

54. Play not the Peacock, looking every where about you, to See if you be well Deck't, if your Shoes fit well if your Stoking Sit neatly, and Cloths handsomely.

55. Eat not in the Streets, nor in ye House, out of Season.

56. Associate yourself with Men of good Quality if you Esteem your own Reputation; for 'tis better to be alone than in bad Company.

57. In walking up and Down in a House, only with One in Compan[y] if he be Greater than yourself, at the first give him the Right hand and Stop not till he does and be not the first that turns, and when you do turn let it be with your face towards him, if he be a Man of Great Quality, walk not with him Cheek by Joul but Somewhat behind him; but yet in Such a Manner that he may easily Speak to you.

58. Let your Conversation be without Malice or Envy, for 'tis a Sig[n o]f a Tractable and Commendable Nature: And in all Causes of Passion [ad]mit Reason to Govern.

59. Never express anything unbecoming, nor Act agst ye Rules Mora[l] before your inferiours.

60. Be not immodest in urging your Freinds to Discover a Secret.

61. Utter not base and frivilous things amongst grave and Learn'd Men nor very Difficult Questians or Subjects, among the Ignorant or things hard to be believed, Stuff not your Discourse with Sentences amongst your Betters nor Equals.

62. Speak not of doleful Things in a Time of Mirth or at the Table; Speak not of Melancholy Things as Death and Wounds, and if others Mention them Change if you can the Discourse tell not your Dreams, but to your intimate Friend.

63. A Man o[ug]ht not to value himself of his Atchievements, or rare Qua[lities of wit; much less of his rich]es Virtue or Kindred.

64. Break not a Jest where none take pleasure in mirth Laugh not aloud, nor at all without Occasion, deride no mans Misfortune, tho' there Seem to be Some cause.

65. Speak not injurious Words neither in Jest nor Earnest Scoff at none although they give Occasion.

66. Be not froward but friendly and Courteous; the first to Salute hear and answer & be not Pensive when it's a time to Converse.

67. Detract not from others neither be excessive in Commanding.

68. Go not thither, where you know not, whether you Shall be Welcome or not. Give not Advice with[out] being Ask'd & when desired [d]o it briefly.

69. If two contend together take not the part of either unconstrain[ed]; and be not obstinate in your own Opinion, in Things indifferent be of the Major Side.

70. Reprehend not the imperfections of others for that belong[s] to Parents Masters and Superiours.

71. Gaze not on the marks or blemishes of Others and ask not how they came. What you may Speak in Secret to your Friend deliver not before others.

72. Speak not in an unknown Tongue in Company but in your own Language and that as those of Quality do and not as ye Vulgar; Sublime matters treat Seriously.

73. Think before you Speak pronounce not imperfectly nor bring ou[t] your Words too hastily but orderly & distinctly.

74. When Another Speaks be attentive your Self and disturb not the Audience if any hesitate in his Words help him not nor Prompt him without desired, Interrupt him not, nor Answer him till his Speec[h] be ended.

75. In the midst of Discourse ask [not of what one treateth] but if you Perceive any Stop because of [your coming you may well intreat him gently] to Proceed: If a Person of Quality comes in while your Conversing it's handsome to Repeat what was said before.

76. While you are talking, Point not with your Finger at him of Whom you Discourse nor Approach too near him to whom you talk especially to his face.

77. Treat with men at fit Times about Business & Whisper not in the Company of Others.

78. Make no Comparisons and if any of the Company be Commended for any brave act of Vertue, commend not another for the Same.

79. Be not apt to relate News if you know not the truth thereof. In Discoursing of things you Have heard Name not your Author always A [Se]cret Discover not.

80. Be not Tedious in Discourse or in reading unless you find the Company pleased therewith.

81. Be not Curious to Know the Affairs of Others neither approach those that Speak in Private.

82. Undertake not what you cannot Perform but be Carefull to keep your Promise.

83. When you deliver a matter do it without Passion & with Discretion, howev[er] mean the Person be you do it too.

84. When your Superiours talk to any Body hearken not neither Speak nor Laugh.

85. In the Company of these of Higher Quality than yourself Speak not ti[l] you are ask'd a Question then Stand upright put of[f] your Hat & Answer in few words.

86. In Disputes, be not So Desireous to Overcome as not to give Liberty to each one to deliver his Opinion and Submit to ye Judgment of ye Major Part especially if they are Judges of the Dispute.

87. [Let your carriage be such] as becomes a Man Grave Settled and attentive [to that which is spoken. Contra]dict not at every turn what others Say.

88. Be not tedious in Discourse, make not many Digressions, nor rep[eat] often the Same manner of Discourse.

89. Speak not Evil of the absent for it is unjust.

90. Being Set at meat Scratch not neither Spit Cough or blow your Nose except there's a Necessity for it.

91. Make no Shew of taking great Delight in your Victuals, Feed no[t] with Greediness; cut your Bread with a Knife, lean not on the Table neither find fault with what you Eat.

92. Take no Salt or cut Bread with your Knife Greasy.

93. Entertaining any one at table it is decent to present him wt. meat, Undertake not to help others undesired by ye Master.

94. If you Soak bread in the Sauce let it be no more than what you [pu]t in your Mouth at a time and blow not your broth at Table [bu]t Stay till Cools of it Self.

95. Put not your meat to your Mouth with your Knife in your ha[nd ne]ither Spit forth the Stones of any fruit Pye upon a Dish nor Cas[t an]ything under the table.

96. It's unbecoming to Stoop much to ones Meat Keep your Fingers clea[n &] when foul wipe them on a Corner of your Table Napkin.

97. Put not another bit into your Mouth til the former be Swallowed [l]et not your Morsels be too big for the Jouls.

98. Drink not nor talk with your mouth full neither Gaze about you while you are a Drinking.

99. Drink not too leisurely nor yet too hastily. Before and after Drinking wipe your Lips breath not then or Ever with too Great a Noise, for its uncivil.

100. Cleanse not your teeth with the Table Cloth Napkin Fork or Knife but if Others do it let it be done wt. a Pick Tooth.

101. Rince not your Mouth in the Presence of Others.

102. It is out of use to call upon the Company often to Eat...

103. In company of your Betters be no[t longer in eating] than they are lay not your Arm but o[nly your hand upon the table].

104. It belongs to ye Chiefest in Company to unfold his Napkin and fall to Meat first, But he ought then to Begin in time & to Dispatch [w]ith Dexterity that ye Slowest may have time allowed him.

105. Be not Angry at Table whatever happens & if you have reason to be so, Shew it not but on a Chearfull Countenance especially if there be Strangers for Good Humour makes one Dish of Meat a Feas[t].

106. Set not yourself at ye upper of ye Table but if it Be your Due or that ye Master of ye house will have it So, Contend not, least you Should Trouble ye Company.

107. If others talk at Table be attentive but talk not with Meat in your Mouth.

108. When you Speak of God or his Atributes, let it be Seriously & [wt] Reverence. Honour & Obey your Natural Parents altho they be Poor.

109. Let your Recreations be Manful not Sinfull.

110. Labour to keep alive in your Breast that Little Spark of Ce[les]tial fire Called Conscience.

Finis

On Christmas Day

Assist me Muse divine! to Sing the Morn,
On which the Saviour of Mankind was born;
But oh! what Numbers to the Theme can rise?
Unless kind Angels aid me from the Skies!
Methinks I see the tunefull Host descend,
And with officious Joy the Scene attend!
Hark, by their Hymns directed on the Road,
The Gladsome Shepherd's find the Nascent God!
And view the Infant conscious of his Birth,
Smiling bespeak Salvation to the Earth!

      For when the important Æra first drew near
for which the great Messiah Should appear;
And to accomplish his redeeming Love,
Resign a while his glorious Throne above;
Beneath our Form should every Woe Sustain,
And by triumphant Suffering fix his Reign,
Should for lost Man in Tortures yield his Breath
Dying to save us from eternal Death!
Oh my stick union!—Salutary Grace!
Incarnate God our Nature should embrace!
That Deity should stoop to our Disguise!
That man recovered should regain the skies!
Dejected adam! from thy grave ascend,
And view the Serpants Deadly Malice end;
Adoring bless th' Almighty's boundless Grace
That gave his son a Ransome for thy Race!
Oh never let my Soul this Day forget,
But pay in graitfull praise her annual Debt
To him, whom 'tis my Trust, I Shall [adore]
When Time, and Sin, and Death, [shall be no more!]

The tangled threads from our view of underneath the tapestry appear to be in disarray, but do not be dismayed. The Designer of the family has been at work weaving with expertise from above. He turns His masterpiece over and a work of meticulous beauty is portrayed in a silken garden. Having faith in God's Word, the Holy Bible is depicted in buds of violet while living by godly principles is represented by sprouts of emerald. Enduring hardships is shown in deep crimson whereas having perseverance is popping out in knots of silver. Respecting parental authority is revealed in the blossoms of a rose along with loving truth pictured in lines of gold. Performing physical exercise is bursting out in leaves of turquoise, loving to learn is entwined in fuchsia, and learning to work is seen in the velvet backdrop of hunter green. All these silken threads are woven throughout the families of Washington, Lincoln, and many others of early America.

Families in America who put these foundational truths to the test were rewarded with beautiful memories. These truths are still at work today in the United States of America making strong families who, in turn, make a stronger nation for the next generation.

Chapter Four

Foundations of Faith

United States Capitol Building

During mankind's history, nations have built great monuments to honor or to commemorate valor, ideologies, and beliefs of every description. America's monuments, memorials, and public buildings in Washington, D.C. have a common thread portraying a trust in God and in the Holy Bible. This belief system, based upon trusting God, is the foundation of faith upon which the United States of America was established. America's national government proclaimed a trust in God which is reflected in her founding documents. This belief and foundation of faith is also America's national motto, *In God We Trust*. It is displayed in many of the buildings on Capitol Hill. In America's Capitol building there are eight massive paintings; half of them are dedicated to the Age of Exploration and Discovery, and the other half are dedicated to the War for Independence. Three of these painting have a direct correlation to America's foundation of faith in God.

Landing of Columbus

The Landing of Columbus shows a man's faith in God's direction. Columbus states in his journal that he was motivated to make the hazardous trip because *it was the Lord Who put it into my mind*. Columbus trusted in God as his Divine Navigator.

Embarkation of the Pilgrims

The Embarkation of the Pilgrims depicts a unified faith in God's promises. The Separatists on the deck of the *Speedwell*, July 22 of 1620, in South Holland are kneeling in prayer while William Brewster is holding an opened Bible. A sail, with the words *God with us*, is blowing in the breeze while a rainbow, symbolizing Divine mercy and grace, is overshadowing them. The Separatists trusted in God as their Captain of the ship.

The Baptism of Pocahontas

The Baptism of Pocahontas illustrates a believing faith in God's salvation. Pocahontas accepted Christianity from her interaction with the Gospel in the Virginia Colony. From the First Charter of Virginia were these words penned: *We, greatly commending, and graciously accepting of, their Desires for the Furtherance of so noble a Work, which may, by the Providence of Almighty God, hereafter tend to the Glory of his Divine Majesty, in propagating of Christian Religion to such People, as yet live in Darkness and miserable Ignorance of the true Knowledge and Worship of God...*

John Winthrop

Roger Williams

George Washington

Samuel Adams

Peter Muhlenberg

Jonathan Trumbull

Robert E. Lee

Lew Wallace

Daniel Webster

James Garfield

There are many statues in the Capitol of notable individuals; the majority are Christians who did great things by trusting in God: John Winthrop, Roger Williams, George Washington, Samuel Adams, Peter Muhlenberg, Jonathan Trumbull, Daniel Webster, Lew Wallace, Robert E. Lee, and James Garfield; to name a few.

When one walks through the National Mall of Washington, D.C., it is readily evident the city was birthed and was designed by men who had a firm reliance upon God and upon the Holy Bible. Everywhere etched in granite, in marble, and in stone is the national motto, *In God We Trust*, and other references to God and the Holy Bible.

Psalm 33:12 *Blessed is the nation whose God is the Lord; and the people whom he hath chosen for his own inheritance.*

The settlers of the United States of America came to these shores with a common vision predicated upon their trust in God. The founders came to America driven by a sense of destiny, an unstoppable plan of action based upon a belief system of their faith that had been instilled in them very carefully from generations past. They had learned how to apply God's Word to the world in which they lived. The world's foundation rests upon God's law, written down in God's Holy Word, the Bible; God's history (His story). The founders exemplified God's truth as living epistles to the principles upon that trust in God which is the foundation of America.

The Bible clearly shows that the nation of Israel trusted in God and because of that trust, He performed miracles for them. America has also trusted in God as a nation. That national trust in God moved God to perform the miraculous for America from the settling of the New World to the birth of America. From the battlefields of the War for Independence to the halls of legislatures, God's miracles moved upon America because of America's trust in God.

I Kings 8:57-58 *The Lord our God be with us, as he was with our fathers: let him not leave us, nor forsake us: That he may incline our hearts unto him, to walk in all his ways, and to keep his commandments, and his statutes, and his judgments, which he commanded our fathers.*

*Signing of the Declaration of Independence
of the United States of America*

The signers of the Declaration of Independence justified their separation with England by citing the laws of nature and of nature's God as stated in the following two verses:

Psalm 19:1 *The heavens declare the glory of God; and the firmament sheweth his handywork.*

Romans 1:20 *For the invisible things of him from the creation of the world are clearly seen, being understood by the things that are made, even his eternal power and Godhead; so that they are without excuse:*

The signers of the Declaration of Independence appealed to the Supreme Judge of the world for the rectitude of their intentions. Their secret was a humble relationship with and a trust in the God of the Holy Bible; not a trust in their wealth, education, or station in life; but what George Washington called, *The eternal rules of right.* They realized success in life started from trusting in the source of life, JEHOVAH GOD, and they also realized all men are created equal and are endowed by their Creator with certain unalienable rights...life, liberty, and the pursuit of happiness.

The Founding Fathers had a close walk with God, and worshipped Him allowing them to found a nation and to win their liberty by trusting in God and not in man.

Psalm 118:8-9 *It is better to trust in the Lord than to put confidence in man. It is better to trust in the Lord than to put confidence in princes.*

The Founding Fathers personified this when they said, *With a firm reliance on the protection of divine Providence we mutually pledge to each other our lives, our fortunes, and our sacred honor.* They received strength from the LORD to endure the eight-year War for Independence.

Isaiah 26:4 *Trust ye in the Lord for ever: for in the Lord Jehovah is everlasting strength:*

Bombardment of Fort McHenry

Francis Scott Key

Francis Scott Key Monument
Baltimore, MD

DEFENCE OF FORT M'HENRY.

The annexed song was composed under the following circumstances—
A gentleman had left Baltimore, in a flag of truce for the purpose of get-
ting released from the British fleet, a friend of his who had been captured
at Marlborough.—He went as far as the mouth of the Patuxent, and was
not permitted to return lest the intended attack on Baltimore should be
disclosed. He was therefore brought up the Bay to the mouth of the Pa-
tapsco, where the flag vessel was kept under the guns of a frigate, and
he was compelled to witness the bombardment of Fort M'Henry, which
the Admiral had boasted that he would carry in a few hours, and
that the city must fall. He watched the flag at the Fort through the
whole day with an anxiety that can be better felt than described, until
the night prevented him from seeing it. In the night he watched the Bomb
Shells, and at early dawn his eye was again greeted by the proudly waving
flag of his country.

TUNE—ANACREON IN HEAVEN.

O! say can you see by the dawn's early light,
   What so proudly we hailed at the twilight's last gleaming,
Whose broad stripes and bright stars through the perilous fight,
   O'er the ramparts we watch'd, were so gallantly streaming?
And the Rockets' red glare, the Bombs bursting in air,
Gave proof through the night that our Flag was still there;
      O! say does that star-spangled Banner yet wave,
      O'er the Land of the free, and the home of the brave?

On the shore dimly seen through the mists of the deep,
   Where the foe's haughty host in dread silence reposes,
What is that which the breeze, o'er the towering steep,
   As it fitfully blows, half conceals, half discloses?
Now it catches the gleam of the morning's first beam,
In full glory reflected now shines in the stream,
      'Tis the star spangled banner, O! long may it wave
      O'er the land of the free and the home of the brave.

And where is that band who so vauntingly swore
   That the havoc of war and the battle's confusion,
A home and a country, shall leave us no more?
   Their blood has washed out their foul footsteps pollution,
No refuge could save the hireling and slave,
From the terror of flight or the gloom of the grave,
      And the star-spangled banner in triumph doth wave,
      O'er the Land of the Free, and the Home of the Brave.

O! thus be it ever when freemen shall stand,
   Between their lov'd home, and the war's desolation,
Blest with vict'ry and peace, may the Heav'n rescued land,
   Praise the Power that hath made and preserv'd us a nation!
Then conquer we must, when our cause it is just,
And this be our motto—"In God is our Trust;"
      And the star-spangled Banner in triumph shall wave,
      O'er the Land of the Free, and the Home of the Brave.

1814 Broadside Printing of the Defence of Fort McHenry
(This poem later became the national anthem of the United States of America.)

103

The First Printing of The Star Spangled Banner

By a Congressional resolution on March 3, 1931, the *Star Spangled Banner* was adopted as the national anthem for America. It was written by Francis Scott Key during the War of 1812. The motto, *In God We Trust*, came from part of a stanza in the *Star Spangled Banner* Key had written on September 13-14, 1814 while watching the bombardment of Fort McHenry during a prisoner-exchange negotiation upon the British ship, HMS *Tonnant*, two years into the War of 1812.

O thus be it ever, when free men shall stand
Between their loved homes and the war's desolation!
Blest with vict'ry and peace, may the heav'n-rescued land
Praise the Pow'r that hath made and preserved us a nation!
Then conquer we must, when our cause it is just;
And this be our motto: In God is our Trust!
And the star-spangled banner in triumph shall wave
O'er the land of the free and the home of the brave!

This national anthem was born out of darkness and danger, but in the morning the flag was still there. The American government took the phrase, *In God is our Trust*, and reworded it as *In God We Trust* making it the motto for America.

Psalm 22:4-5 *Our fathers trusted in thee: they trusted, and thou didst deliver them. They cried unto thee, and were delivered: they trusted in thee, and were not confounded.*

The Speaker's Rostrum in the U.S. House of Representatives

The motto, *In God We Trust,* is etched in the national history of the United States. This motto of the United States of America is displayed above the speaker's rostrum in the U.S. House of Representatives, and is displayed at the entrance to the Capitol Visitor's Center, at the south door of the senate, on a tribute block on the Washington Monument, on the east wall of the Longworth Building, at the southwest entrance in the Derksen Office Building, and on a stained-glass panel in the chapel of the Capitol.

Stained Glass in the Chapel of the United States Capitol

During a ceremony, on April 8, 1954, commemorating the first stamp with *In God We Trust*, President Eisenhower said : *America's greatness has been based upon a spiritual quality symbolized by the stamp. He also said, Here is the land that lives in the respect for the Almighty's mercy to us, each individual affixing this stamp on the letter cannot fail to feel something of the inspiration whenever we read [In God we Trust].* That same day Eisenhower said at a women's conference, *I just came from a dedication of the new stamp...all of us mere mortals are dependent upon the mercy of a Superior being, every individual that uses this stamp sends a message that this is the land of the free and the home of the brave because [In God We Trust].*

Official White House Portrait of Dwight D. Eisenhower

President Eisenhower stated at the *75th Anniversary of the Incandescent Lamp*, October 24, 1954: *Atheism substitutes men for the Supreme Creator and this leads inevitably to domination and dictatorship...It is because we believe that God intends all men to be free and equal that we demand free government. Our Government is servant, not master, our chosen representatives are our equals, not our czars or commissars.*

The foundation in faith must be jealously guarded for on it rests the ability of the American individual to live and to thrive in America enabling that one to help others less fortunate to achieve freedom and individual opportunity. Freedom is often taken for granted for those who have attained it, but to others it is often only a wistful dream.

Isaiah 26:2 *Open ye the gates, that the righteous nation which keepeth the truth may enter in. Thou wilt keep him in perfect peace, whose mind is stayed on thee:because he trusteth in thee. Trust ye in the Lord for ever: for in the Lord Jehovah is everlasting strength:*

Noah Webster

The foundation of all free government and all social order must be laid in families and in the discipline of youth. Young persons must not only be furnished with knowledge, but they must be accustomed to subordination and subjected to the authority and influence of good principles. It will avail little that youths are made to understand truth and correct principles, unless they are accustomed to submit to be governed by them...And any system of education...which limits instruction to the arts and sciences, and rejects the aids of religion in forming the character of citizens, is essentially defective. - Noah Webster

No truth is more evident to my mind than that the Christian religion must be the basis of any government intended to secure the rights and privileges of a free people...When I speak of the Christian religion as the basis of government...I mean the primitive Christianity in its simplicity as taught by Christ and His apostles, consisting of a belief in the being, perfections, and government of God; in the revelation of His will to men, as their supreme rule of action; in man's... accountability to God for his conduct in this life; and in the indispensable obligation of all men to yield entire obedience to God's commands in the moral law and the Gospel. - Noah Webster

Thomas Jefferson

The God who gave us life, gave us liberty. - Thomas Jefferson

There are only two nations which began from the truth of God and from the Holy Bible: Israel and the United States of America. All other God-fearing nations had to come to the truth in God. America has been blessed with the heritage of starting with a Christian foundation. Americans must always remember this and keep their trust in God. What is America putting her hope in these days?

Psalm 20:7 *Some trust in chariots, and some in horses: but we will remember the name of the Lord our God.*

On March 3, 1865 the Speaker of the House adopted the phrase, *In God We Trust*. The last act of Congress signed by President Lincoln declared that *In God We Trust* be inscribed on all the national coins. These acts suggest it is essential for America to be reminded daily her trust must be in God and not in her economy.

Psalm 62:10 *Trust not in oppression, and become not vain in robbery: if riches increase, set not your heart upon them.*

Psalm 49:6-7 *They that trust in their wealth, and boast themselves in the multitude of their riches; None of them can by any means redeem his brother, nor give to God a ransom for him:*

America is the wealthiest of all the nations in the world which is a reflection of God's blessings as attested to in Isaiah 26:15a, *Thou hast increased the nation, O Lord.* America's wealth will greatly diminish if her trust in God decreases. Job 12:23 gives a warning for all nations, *He increaseth the nations, and destroyeth them: he enlargeth the nations, and straiteneth them again.*

I pledge allegiance to the Flag of the United States of America, and to the Republic for which it stands, one Nation under God, indivisible, with liberty and justice for all.

On July 11, 1954, a month after the phrase, *under God*, was added to the *Pledge of Allegiance*; Congress enacted *Public Law 84-140* placing the motto on all national currency.

In 1956, *In God We Trust* was adopted by Congress as the official United States' national motto. John F. Kennedy stated February 9, 1961: *The guiding principle of this Nation has been, is now, and ever shall be [IN GOD WE TRUST].*

John F. Kennedy

President Ronald Reagan stated in his *National Day of Prayer Proclamation*, March 19, 1981: *Our Nation's motto [IN GOD WE TRUST]—was not chosen lightly. It reflects a basic recognition that there is a divine authority in the universe to which this Nation owes homage.*

Ronald Reagan

Reagan stated at a White House observance of the National Day of Prayer, May 6, 1982: *Our faith in God is a mighty source of strength. Our Pledge of Allegiance states that we are [one nation under God], and our currency bears the motto, [IN GOD WE TRUST].*

Psalm 44:6-10 *For I will not trust in my bow, neither shall my sword save me. But thou hast saved us from our enemies, and hast put them to shame that hated us. In God we boast all the day long, and praise thy name for ever. Selah. But thou hast cast off, and put us to shame; and goest not forth with our armies. Thou makest us to turn back from the enemy: and they which hate us spoil for themselves.*

America is a nation with her historical foundations resting firmly on faith in God and the Holy Bible as visibly evidenced throughout Washington, D.C. and as remembered in American history.

Isaiah 26:2-4 *Open ye the gates, that the righteous nation which keepeth the truth may enter in. Thou wilt keep him in perfect peace, whose mind is stayed on thee: because he trusteth in thee. Trust ye in the Lord for ever: for in the Lord Jehovah is everlasting strength.*

George Washington said, *Let us raise a standard to which the wise and honest can repair; the rest is in the hands of God.*

Our prayer is that many Americans will begin to rally under the American standard of the foundations of faith to reclaim and to proclaim America's national motto, *In God We Trust.*

Isaiah 58:12 *And they that shall be of thee shall build the old waste places: thou shalt raise up the foundations of many generations; and thou shalt be called, The repairer of the breach, The restorer of paths to dwell in.*

May this American generation be known as the repairers of the breach, restoring the paths, *that the generation to come might know them, even the children which should be born; who should arise and declare them to their children: that they might set their hope in God, and not forget the works of God, but keep his commandments.* Psalm 78:6,7

IN GOD WE TRUST!

Chapter Five

Foundations
of the Federal Government

Scene at the Signing of the Constitution of the United States

Howard Chandler Christy (1940)
United States House of Representatives, Washington, D.C.

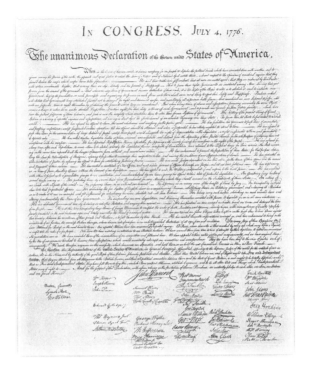

The Declaration of Independence of the United States of America

The Declaration of the original thirteen colonies declared to the community of nations that King George III of Great Britain was violating his own laws and was not fulfilling his responsibilities to his subjects in the American Colonies. For this reason the American Colonies organized themselves as the United States of America and listed grievances toward the crown under international law and appealed to the Supreme Judge of the world for the rectitude of their intentions. These 56 men who were brilliant, were cultured, were wealthy and were settled in reputation and character chose liberty over luxury. They signed a document that was high treason against one of the most powerful monarchs on earth because their allegiance was to a higher King than the king of England. One of the mottos of the War for Independence was "No King but King Jesus".

King George III

The foundation of the War for Independence was as John Adams said, "The general principles on which the Fathers achieved independence were the general principles of Christianity."

The Founding Fathers very specifically wrote that "We hold these Truths to be self-evident, that all Men are created equal, that they are endowed by their Creator with certain unalienable Rights, that among these are Life, Liberty, and the pursuit of Happiness..."

Speaking of *life*, it says in Genesis 2:7, *And the LORD God formed man of the dust of the ground, and breathed into his nostrils the breath of life; and man became a living soul.*

Speaking of *liberty*, it says in 2 Corinthians 3:17, *Now the Lord is that Spirit: and where the Spirit of the Lord is, there is liberty.*

Speaking of *the pursuit of happiness*, it says in Ecclesiastes 3:13, *And also that every man should eat and drink, and enjoy the good of all his labour, it is the gift of God.*

Ecclesiastes 5:19 says, *Every man also to whom God hath given riches and wealth, and hath given him power to eat thereof, and to take his portion, and to rejoice in his labour; this is the gift of God.*

The founding documents of the United States of America clearly express that these rights received are from God. There is a movement today in America to eradicate the God of the Holy Bible from her national consciousness by attempting to take the words *under God* from out of the pledge to the American flag; by attempting to take the words *IN GOD WE TRUST* from off of American currency; and by attempting to take God out of American history in her schools and in her culture. If those factions within American society and within American government can persuade the national populace that it is they who give the rights of *life, liberty,* and *the pursuit of happiness* to the American people, and not the God of the Holy Bible; they will then have the power to take those rights away from the citizens of the United States of America.

Because of its divine design, the United States Constitution has given America the most unique, powerful, and benevolent nation in modern history.

James Madison

We have staked the whole future of American civilization, not upon the power of government, far from it. We've staked the future of all our political institutions upon our capacity...to sustain ourselves according to the Ten Commandments of God. 1778 James Madison to the General Assembly of the State of Virginia.

In the Kentucky Resolutions of 1798: Thomas Jefferson stated...*in questions of power then, let no more be heard of confidence in man, but bind him down from mischief by the chains of the constitution...*

National Archives Building, Washington, D.C.

Housed in the National Archives building in Washington, D.C. is the most important, legal document in United States' history. It is the most miraculous, governmental document in the history of mankind. It is the road map, a blueprint, by which the American government is to be operated; a formula for national success that if any nation would follow, could produce a Biblical standard of government and thereby obtain liberty and great prosperity. The Constitution is the document that completes the infrastructure of the Declaration of Independence. Based upon the Bible this document has not just granted, but has guaranteed the American people certain unalienable, God-given rights being life, liberty, and the pursuit of happiness.

*A Portion of the Constitution of the
United States of America*

The design of the Constitution of the United States goes far beyond the collective genius of the American Founding Fathers. The impetus for the Constitution is divine in its origin. At the Constitutional Convention of 1787, James Madison proposed the plan to divide the central government into three branches. He discovered this model of government from the Perfect Governor as he read Isaiah 33:22. *For the LORD is our judge, the LORD is our lawgiver, the LORD is our king; He will save us.*

Baron Charles Montesquieu

Baron Charles Montesquieu wrote in 1748, *Nor is there liberty if the power of judging is not separated from legislative power and from executive power. If it [the power of judging] were joined to legislative power, the power over life and liberty of the citizens would be arbitrary, for the judge would be the legislature if it were joined to the executive power, the judge could have the force of an oppressor. All would be lost if the same...body of principal men...exercised these three powers.* Madison claimed Isaiah 33:22 as the source of division of power in government.

William Gladstone

William Gladstone who was a former, prime minister of Great Britain said, *The American Constitution is, so far as I can see, the most wonderful work ever struck off at a given time by the brain and purpose of man.*

The reason why legal scholars have marveled at the scope, resilience, and timeless strength of the Constitution is because, in this author's opinion, its design goes beyond human capacity. The American Founding Fathers were asking for God's guidance and were referring to His ultimate book of law, the Holy Bible, for its principles. They incorporated over twenty Biblical principles in the Constitution. It would serve the people of the United States well to learn these principles themselves and then instill them once again into the hearts of their leadership and in the halls of the American government.

The following 28 foundational principles were derived from the Bible and incorporated by the Founding Fathers into the Constitution. These principles must be understood and perpetuated by every American citizen so that generations to come may find peace, prosperity, and freedom in the United States of America.

Principle 1 - The only reliable basis for sound government and just human relations is natural law.

Natural law is God's law. There are certain laws which govern the entire universe and, just as Thomas Jefferson said in the Declaration of Independence, there are laws which govern in the affairs of men which are the *laws of nature and of nature's God.*

Psalm 19:1 *The heavens declare the glory of God; and the firmament sheweth his handywork.*

Romans 1:20 *For the invisible things of him from the creation of the world are clearly seen, being understood by the things that are made, even his eternal power and Godhead; so that they are without excuse:*

Principle 2 - A free people cannot survive under a republican constitution unless they remain virtuous and morally strong.

Benjamin Franklin

Only a virtuous people are capable of freedom. As nations become corrupt and vicious, they have more need of masters. - Benjamin Franklin

Proverbs 14:34 *Righteousness exalteth a nation: but sin is a reproach to any people.*

Americans with faith in the God of the Holy Bible must be the conscience of America reminding her leaders and her citizens why she is blessed in so many ways.

Principle 3 - The most promising method of securing a virtuous people is to elect virtuous leaders.

Neither the wisest constitution nor the wisest laws will secure the liberty and happiness of a people whose manners are universally corrupt. He therefore is the truest friend to the liberty of his country who tries most to promote its virtue, and who...will not suffer a man to be chosen into any office of power and trust who is not a wise and virtuous man. - Samuel Adams

Proverbs 29:2 *When the righteous are in authority, the people rejoice: but when the wicked beareth rule, the people mourn*

Now more than ever before, the people are responsible for the character of their Congress. If that body be ignorant, reckless and corrupt, it is because the people tolerate ignorance, recklessness and corruption. If it be intelligent, brave and pure, it is because the people demand these high qualities to represent them in the national legislature...If the next centennial does not find us a great nation...it will be because those who represent the enterprise, the culture, and the morality of the nation do not aid in controlling the political forces. - President James A. Garfield

Principle 4 - Without religion, the government of a free people cannot be maintained.

Psalm 9:17 *The wicked shall be turned into hell, and all the nations that forget God.*

Of all the dispositions and habits which lead to political prosperity; religion and morality are indispensable supports...And let us with caution indulge the supposition that morality can be maintained without religion. - George Washington

Principle 5 - All things were created by God, therefore upon Him all mankind are equally dependent, and to Him they are equally responsible.

Colossians 1:16 *For by him were all things created, that are in heaven, and that are in earth, visible and invisible, whether they be thrones, or dominions, or principalities, or powers: all things were created by him, and for him*

The American Founding Fathers considered the existence of the Creator as the most fundamental premise underlying all self-evident truth. They felt a person who boasted that he or she was an atheist had just simply failed to apply his or her divine capacity for reason and observation.

Principle 6 - All mankind were created equal.

Genesis 1:27 *So God created man in his own image, in the image of God created he him; male and female created he them.*

The American Founding Fathers knew all mankind are theoretically treated as:

Equal before God.
Equal before the law.
Equal in their rights.

Principle 7 - The proper role of government is to protect equal rights, not provide equal things.

The American Founding Fathers recognized the people cannot delegate to their government any power except that which they have the lawful right to exercise themselves.

Principle 8 - Mankind is endowed by God with certain unalienable rights.

Genesis 2:7 *And the Lord God formed man of the dust of the ground, and breathed into his nostrils the breath of life; and man became a living soul.*

2 Corinthians 3:17 *Now the Lord is that Spirit: and where the Spirit of the Lord is, there is liberty.*

Ecclesiastes 3:13, *And also that every man should eat and drink, and enjoy the good of all his labour, it is the gift of God.*

Ecclesiastes 5:19 says, *Every man also to whom God hath given riches and wealth, and hath given him power to eat thereof, and to take his portion, and to rejoice in his labour; this is the gift of God.*

William Blackstone

Those rights, then, which God and nature have established, and are therefore called natural rights, such as are life and liberty, need not the aid of human laws to be more effectually invested in every man than they are; neither do they receive any additional strength when declared by the municipal [or state] laws to be inviolable. On the contrary, no human legislation has power to abridge or destroy them, unless the owner [of the right] shall himself commit some act that amounts to a forfeiture. - William Blackstone

Principle 9 - To protect human rights, God has revealed a code of divine law.

Leviticus 22:31 *Therefore shall ye keep my commandments, and do them: I am the Lord.*

The doctrines thus delivered we call the revealed or divine law, and they are to be found only in the Holy Scriptures. These precepts, when revealed, are found by comparison to be really a part of the original law of nature, as they tend in all their consequences to man's felicity. - William Blackstone

Principle 10 - The God-given right to govern is vested in the sovereign authority of the whole people.

Alexander Hamilton

The fabric of American empire ought to rest on the solid basis of the consent of the people. The streams of national power ought to flow immediately from that pure, original fountain of all legislative authority. - Alexander Hamilton

Principle 11 - The majority of the people may alter or abolish a government which has become tyrannical.

Prudence, indeed, will dictate that governments long established should not be changed for light and transient causes...but when a long train of abuses and usurpations...evinces a design to reduce them under absolute despotism, it is their right, it is their duty, to throw off such government, and to provide new guards for their future security. - Thomas Jefferson in the Declaration of Independence

Principle 12 - The United States of America shall be a republic.

Exodus 18:25 *And Moses chose able men out of all Israel, and made them heads over the people, rulers of thousands, rulers of hundreds, rulers of fifties, and rulers of tens.*

Nowhere in the Constitution does it mention the word *democracy*, but in Article IV, Section 4, it states, *The United States shall guarantee to every State in this Union a Republican Form of Government...*

When American citizens pledge to the American flag, it is not *to the Democracy for which it stands, but to the Republic for which it stands. I pledge allegiance to the flag of the United States of America, and to the Republic for which it stands...*

Principle 13 - A constitution should protect the people from the frailties of their rulers.

Jeremiah 17:9 *The heart is deceitful above all things, and desperately wicked: who can know it?*

If angels were to govern men, neither external nor internal controls on government would be necessary...[But lacking these] you must first enable the government to control the governed; and in the next place oblige it to control itself. - James Madison

This is the reasoning behind America having a separation of powers. If one branch of the government goes astray, the other two can correct it through legal recourse.

Principle 14 - Life and liberty are secure only so long as the rights of property are secure.

1 Kings 21:3 *And Naboth said to Ahab, The Lord forbid it me, that I should give the inheritance of my fathers unto thee.*

John Locke

John Locke reasoned that God gave the earth and everything in it to the whole human family as a gift. Therefore the land, the sea, the acorns in the forest, and the deer feeding in the meadow all belong to everyone *in common*. However, the moment someone takes the trouble to change something from its original state of nature, that person has added his ingenuity or labor to make that change. Herein lies the secret to the origin of *property rights*.

The moment the idea is admitted into society, that property is not as sacred as the laws of God, and there is not a force of law and public justice to protect it, anarchy and tyranny commence. If [Thou shalt not covet], and [Thou shalt not steal], were not commandments of Heaven, they must be made inviolable precepts in every society, before it can be civilized or made free. John Adams, *Defense of the Constitutions of Government of the United States. The Works of John Adams.* Edited by Charles Francis Adams. 10 vols. Boston: Little, Brown & Co., 1850-1856. See also: Butterfield; Capon: *Warren-Adams Letters*

Principle 15 - The highest level of prosperity occurs when there is a free-market economy and a minimum of government regulations.

Ecclesiastes 5:19 says, *Every man also to whom God hath given riches and wealth, and hath given him power to eat thereof, and to take his portion, and to rejoice in his labour; this is the gift of God.*

Prosperity depends upon a climate of wholesome stimulation by the following four, basic freedoms in operation:

The freedom to try.
The freedom to buy.
The freedom to sell.
The freedom to fail.

Principle 16 - The government should be separated into three branches.

John Adams

I call you to witness that I was the first member of the Congress who ventured to come out in public, as I did in January 1776, in my Thoughts on Government...in favor of a government with three branches and an independent judiciary. This pamphlet, you know, was very unpopular. No man appeared in public to support it but yourself. - John Adams to Benjamin Rush

Principle 17 - A system of checks and balances should be adopted to prevent the abuse of power by the different branches of government.

It will not be denied that power is of an encroaching nature and that it ought to be effectually restrained from passing the limits assigned to it. - James Madison

The accumulation of all powers, Legislative, Executive, and Judiciary, in the same hands, whether of one, a few, or many...may justly be pronounced the very definition of tyranny. - James Madison

Principle 18 - The unalienable rights of the people are most likely to be preserved if the principles of government are set forth in a written constitution.

The structure of the American system is set forth in the Constitution of the United States and the only weaknesses which have appeared are those which were allowed to creep in despite the Constitution.

Principle 19 - Only limited and carefully defined powers should be delegated to government; all others being retained by the people.

The Tenth Amendment is the most widely violated provision of the Bill of Rights. If it had been respected and enforced, America would be an amazingly different country than she is today. This amendment provides:

The powers not delegated to the United States by the Constitution, nor prohibited by it to the States, are reserved to the States respectively, or to the people.

Principle 20 - Efficiency and dispatch require that the government operate according to the will of the majority, but constitutional provisions must be made to protect the rights of the minority.

Every man, by consenting with others to make one body politic under one government, puts himself under an obligation to every one of that society to submit to the determination of the majority, and to be concluded [bound] by it. - John Locke

Principle 21 — Strong, local self-government is the keystone to preserving human freedom.

Thomas Jefferson

The way to have good and safe government is not to trust it all to one, but to divide it among the many, distributing to every one exactly the functions he is competent [to perform best]. - Thomas Jefferson

Principle 22 - A free people should be governed by law and not by the whims of men.

The end of law is not to abolish or restrain, but to preserve and enlarge freedom. For in all the states of created beings, capable of laws, where there is no law there is no freedom. For liberty is to be free from restraint and violence of others, which cannot be where there is no law. - John Locke

Principle 23 - A free society cannot survive as a republic without a broad program of general education.

They made an early provision by law that every town consisting of so many families should be always furnished with a grammar school. They made it a crime for such a town to be destitute of a grammar schoolmaster for a few months, and subjected it to a heavy penalty. So that the education of all ranks of people was made the care and expense of the public, in a manner that I believe has been unknown to any other people, ancient or modern. The consequences of these establishments we see and feel every day [written in 1765]. A native of America who cannot read and write is as rare...as a comet or an earthquake. - John Adams

Principle 24 - A free people will not survive unless they stay strong.

To be prepared for war is one of the most effectual means of preserving peace. - George Washington

Principle 25 - Peace, commerce, and honest friendship with all nations -- entangling alliances with none. - Thomas Jefferson, Given in His <u>First Inaugural Address</u>.

Principle 26 - The core unit which determines the strength of any society is the family; therefore the government should foster and protect its integrity.

Alexis de Tocqueville

There is certainly no country in the world where the tie of marriage is more respected than in America, or where conjugal happiness is more highly or worthily appreciated. - Alexis de Tocqueville

Principle 27 - The burden of debt is as destructive to human freedom as subjugation by conquest.

We are bound to defray expenses [of the war] within our own time, and are unauthorized to burden posterity with them...We shall all consider ourselves morally bound to pay them ourselves and consequently within the life [expectancy] of the majority. - Thomas Jefferson

Principle 28 - The United States has a manifest destiny to eventually become a glorious example of God's law under a restored Constitution that will inspire the entire human race.

(28 Principles used with permission of the National Center for Constitutional Studies.)

The American Founding Fathers sensed from the very beginning they were on a divine mission. Their great disappointment was that it did not all come to pass in their day, but they knew that someday it would come to pass. John Adams wrote, *I always consider the settlement of America with reverence and wonder, as the opening of a grand scene and design in Providence for the illumination of the ignorant, and the emancipation of the slavish part of mankind all over the earth.*

The proof of the success of the United States Constitution is found in how well it has served America. It is the oldest, active constitution in the world today and has proved to be a standard by which the world has measured liberty. George Washington said during the Constitutional Convention, *Let us raise a standard to which the wise and honest can repair; the rest is in the hands of God.* George Washington shaped much of the ideals of the Constitution and the Office of the Executive Branch of the government.

Many do not know the Constitutional Convention was almost a failure. The delegates had argued for five weeks with not much to show for their labors. Half of the people in the United States lived in three states and the other half lived in ten states. Many states had different tariffs and different monetary systems which varied foreign relations. The European powers were salivating over the prospect of this fledgling nation's demise.

George Mason

George Mason, who was a friend of George Washington, got up and walked out of the Constitutional Convention, but George Washington urged him to return by stating that Dr. Franklin was about to speak. Benjamin Franklin, in his eighties and in fragile physical condition, had prepared words summing up the problem with the Constitutional Convention up to that point.

Benjamin Franklin

Mr. President:
The small progress we have made after 4 or 5 weeks close attendance & continual reasonings with each other – our different sentiments on almost every question, several of the last producing as many noes as ayes, is methinks a melancholy proof of the imperfection of the Human Understanding.

We indeed seem to feel our own want of political wisdom, since we have been running about in search of it. We have gone back to ancient history for models of Government, and examined the different forms of those Republics which, having been formed with the seeds of their own dissolution, now no longer exist. And we have viewed Modern States all round Europe, but find none of their Constitutions suitable to our circumstances.

In this situation of this Assembly, groping as it were in the dark to find political truth, and scarce able to distinguish it when presented to us, how has it happened, Sir, that we have not hitherto once thought of humbly applying to the Father of lights to illuminate our understanding?

In the beginning of the Contest with G. Britain, when we were sensible of danger, we had daily prayer in this room for Divine protection. – Our prayers, Sir, were heard, & they were graciously answered. All of us who were engaged in the struggle must have observed frequent instances of a Superintending Providence in our favor. To that kind Providence we owe this happy opportunity of consulting in peace on the means of establishing our future national felicity. And have we now forgotten that powerful Friend? or do we imagine we no longer need His assistance?

I have lived, Sir, a long time, and the longer I live, the more convincing proofs I see of this truth – that God Governs in the affairs of men. And if a sparrow cannot fall to the ground without His notice, is it probable that an empire can rise without His aid?

We have been assured, Sir, in the Sacred Writings, that "except the Lord build the House, they labor in vain that build it." I firmly believe this; and I also believe that without his concurring aid we shall succeed in this political building no better than the Builders of Babel: We shall be divided by our partial local interests; our projects will be confounded, and we ourselves shall become a reproach and bye word down to future ages. And what is worse, mankind may hereafter from this unfortunate instance, despair of establishing Governments by Human wisdom and leave it to chance, war and conquest. I therefore beg leave to move – that henceforth prayers imploring the assistance of Heaven, and its blessing on our deliberations, be held in this Assembly every morning before we proceed to business...

What many people do not understand is that after Dr. Franklin spoke, the delegates recessed for several days. Many prayed, fasted, and attended church services. When the Congress reconvened there was a completely different atmosphere and attitude among the delegates. At the end of the Constitutional Convention, Dr. Franklin again rose to the occasion when he diplomatically exhorted dissenting delegates to put aside their legitimate criticisms (he himself had several) and recognize the version before them as the best compromise possible.

Daniel Webster

Daniel Webster said, *Hold on, my friends, to the Constitution and to the Republic for which it stands. Miracles do not cluster and what has happened once in 6,000 years may not happen again. Hold on to the Constitution, for if the American Constitution should fail, there will be anarchy throughout the world.*

Ronald Reagan

Ronald Reagan said, *Perhaps you and I have lived with this miracle too long to be properly appreciative. Freedom is a fragile thing and is never more than one generation away from extinction. It is not ours by inheritance; it must be fought for and defended constantly by each generation, for it comes only once to a people. Those who have known freedom and then lost it have never known it again.*

Knowing this, it is hard to explain those who even today would question the people's capacity for self rule. Will they answer this: If no one among us is capable of governing himself, then who among us has the capacity to govern someone else? Using the temporary authority granted by the people, an increasing number lately have sought to control the means of production as if this could be done without eventually controlling those who produce. Always this is explained as necessary to the people's welfare. But, "The deterioration of every government begins with the decay of the principle upon which it was founded." This is true today as it was when it was written in 1748.

Many American citizens have never read the United States Constitution, and most do not have a working knowledge of America's owner's manual. The processes of government are very important to its continuance. The United States Constitution is very Biblical in its scope. According to a University of Houston study, thirty-four percent of all quotes of the American Founding Fathers came from the Holy Bible. Another sixty percent of their contributions to the Constitution came from men who used the Bible to form their conclusions. A total of ninety-four percent of all their quotes came either from the Bible itself, or someone indirectly citing the Bible, or Biblical principled quotes. A sad fact is that many Americans do not know that 52 of the 55 framers of the Constitution were avowed Christians. Although Dr. Benjamin Franklin was a deist, one must consider his speech to the delegates at the Constitutional Convention where he Biblically challenged the delegates to pray before going to deliberation each day. Historian C. Gregg Singer points out, *Christian theism had so permeated the colonial mind that it continued to guide even those who had come to regard the Gospel with indifference or even hostility.* Much of the ideology of the Constitution was received from people like William Blackstone, who was very Biblically influenced as evidenced in his many and varied Biblical references in his writings.

The United States Constitution is the supreme law of America; it supersedes all other laws in her land. If there is a law or ideology in America that is contrary to the United States Constitution it must be eradicated out of the American government and out of the lives of her citizens.

The Constitution outlines how the United States government should operate.

*The Legislative Branch** of the government is that body which makes the laws. **Article I, section 1.** *All legislative Powers herein granted shall be vested in a Congress of the United States, which shall consist of a Senate and House of Representatives.*

In my travels across America, I have asked even six-year-olds, "If all legislative powers are vested only in the Congress, how much of that power is left over for the other two branches of government?" Everyone has always been quick to respond that there would be none of the legislative power left for the other two branches of government. So the question I pose to the reader, if all legislative powers in the United States are vested in her Congress, and no other branch has any Constitutional ground for making or negating laws; why is the United States Supreme Court and lesser courts, legislating laws for the United States of America from the bench?

*The Judicial branch of the government only interprets the law. It is up to the legislative branch, which represents *We the People*, to determine if the law should be made, changed or negated.

*The Executive Branch of the government as in Article II, section 3 asserts, *The President shall take care that the laws are faithfully executed...* saying nothing about making or negating a law, as in Executive Orders, but only executing the laws that Congress has made.

Herein lies the problem. *We the People*, do not know the Constitutional rights given to the American people. It is high time the American people learn these rights and incorporate these rights into their daily lives so that they may once again become truly a self-governed people. Electing the right people to represent *We the People* is essential. Even more important than this is the necessity of the American people in knowing the processes of government in order to stay responsibly engaged to support, to pray for, and to hold all those in leadership accountable to America's owner's manual, the United States Constitution.

Convention President's Chair

On the final day of the Constitutional Convention, as the last delegates were signing the document, Franklin pointed toward the sun on the back of the Convention President's chair. Observing the craftsmen had made it difficult to distinguish in their art a rising sun from a setting sun, he went on to say, *I have often…in the course of the session…looked at that sun behind the President without being able to tell whether it was rising or setting. But now at length I have the happiness to know it is a rising and not a setting sun.*

It is now the turn for American citizens to ponder the importance of the United States Constitution which is, in my opinion, the most miraculous, governmental document in the history of mankind. Will it be a setting sun or a rising sun?

Whether the United States of America continues in the time-tested principles upon which she was established, or whether she falters and fails; depends upon, *We the People*. American citizens must read the United States Constitution and ingest its principles so all Americans can do their part to protect, to preserve, and to pass on liberty to America's future generations. May American citizens be found faithful in this regard.

Chapter Six

Foundations of Fidelity

Definition of Fidelity

FIDEL'ITY, *noun* [*Latin fidelitas, from fides, faith, fido, to trust.*]
Faithfulness; careful and exact observance of duty, or performance of obligations.

Noah Webster's 1828 Dictionary

When one applies this truth and serves one's nation from this standpoint, extraordinary and even miraculous things can be accomplished. This truth personified in the heart and mind can affect a nation and generations to come.

James 1:25 says, *But whoso looketh into the perfect law of liberty, and continueth therein, he being not a forgetful hearer, but a doer of the work, this man shall be blessed in his deed.*

America's founders did just that in answering the call of fidelity and became the architects of the United States of America. Those early laborers whom God selected dug deep foundations, toiled with their blood, sweat, and tears; and gave their very lives as bedrock that Americans might live in the greatest nation on earth.

John Witherspoon, a Presbyterian Minister and the President of Princeton University Who Signed the Declaration of Independence

The sum of the whole is that the blessing of God is only to be looked for by those who are not wanting in the discharge of their own duty. - John Witherspoon

Ecclesiastes 12:13 *Let us hear the conclusion of the whole matter: Fear God, and keep his commandments: for this is the whole duty of man.*

Herein lies a two-fold maxim for true joy on earth and in heaven, which stresses the greatness and majesty of God. Herein lies the conclusion of the whole matter; to give your all, serving God and country with purity of action forming a foundation of fidelity with awe, reverence, and wonder in the principles of truth.

To fear God is the beginning of wisdom and knowledge as stated in the following two verses:

Psalm 111:10 *The fear of the Lord is the beginning of wisdom: a good understanding have all they that do his commandments: his praise endureth for ever.*

Proverbs 1:7 *The fear of the Lord is the beginning of knowledge: but fools despise wisdom and instruction.*

God states in the following verses from His Holy Word, the first and second greatest commandments:

Matthew 22:36–40 *Master, which is the great commandment in the law? Jesus said unto him, Thou shalt love the Lord thy God with all thy heart, and with all thy soul, and with all thy mind. This is the first and great commandment. And the second is like unto it, Thou shalt love thy neighbour as thyself. On these two commandments hang all the law and the prophets.*

May this truth be engraved in all our hearts; to follow these two great commandments by loving God and loving others as ourselves.

Luke 17:10 *So likewise ye, when ye shall have done all those things which are commanded you, say, We are unprofitable servants: we have done that which was our duty to do.*

What was the one thing America's Founding Fathers had to do to win their nation? It was to do their duty. They understood what duty was and exercised it.

America's Founding Fathers stated that for every right there is a duty to perform. They understood they had a right to be a self-governing nation, and a duty to be self-governing citizens.

Execution of Captain Nathan Hale

Nathan Hale said, *I only regret that I have but one life to lose for my country.* The motto of America's Founding Fathers was, *Sacrifice above all cost, honor above life.*

Patrick Henry

Patrick Henry said, *The millions of people, armed in the holy cause of liberty, and in such a country as that which we possess, are invincible by any force which our enemy can send against us. Besides, sir, we shall not fight our battles alone.*

There is a just God who presides over the destinies of nations, and who will raise up friends to fight our battles for us. The battle, sir, is not to the strong alone; it is to the vigilant, the active, the brave. Besides, sir, we have no election. If we were base enough to desire it, it is now too late to retire from the contest. There is no retreat but in submission and slavery! Our chains are forged! Their clanking may be heard on the plains of Boston! The war is inevitable--and let it come! I repeat it, sir, let it come.

It is in vain, sir, to extenuate the matter. Gentlemen may cry, Peace, Peace-- but there is no peace. The war is actually begun! The next gale that sweeps from the north will bring to our ears the clash of resounding arms! Our brethren are already in the field! Why stand we here idle? What is it that gentlemen wish? What would they have? Is life so dear, or peace so sweet, as to be purchased at the price of chains and slavery? Forbid it, Almighty God! I know not what course others may take; but as for me, give me liberty or give me death!

George Washington

If I were to put a curse on my worst enemy, it would to be to wish him in my position now. I just do not know what to do. It seems impossible to continue my command in this situation, but if I withdraw, all will be lost. [SOURCE: *George Washington After the Fall of Fort Washington, 1776*]

John Adams

John Adams was asked by his hostess at a festive gathering on one of his diplomatic trips to France, *What do you think about our culture, our painting, poetry, music, architecture, statuary, tapestry, and porcelain?*

His reply was, *I must study politics and war that my sons may have liberty to study mathematics and philosophy. My sons ought to study mathematics and philosophy, geography, natural history, naval architecture, navigation, commerce, and agriculture, in order to give their children a right to study painting, poetry, music, architecture, statuary, tapestry, and porcelain, but I must study politics and war!!!*

So what is duty? Duty is that which a person owes to another, that which a person is bound by; any natural, supernatural, moral or legal obligation to pay, to do, or to perform. Duty is integrity which is performing that which you have been created and designed to do. You think, say, and act all the same way.

Taking the oath

A good definition of duty is found in Psalm 15:4b, *He that sweareth to his own hurt, and changeth not.* There are three truths that epitomize duty. **First of all,** *He that sweareth,* **signifying an oath.**

An oath is a solemn affirmation or declaration made with an appeal to God for the truth of what is affirmed. A man may say these words with a hand raised to God with the meaning that he is making himself accountable to God for this his oath; his pledge. All of our military swear an oath as they begin their service...*I, [name], do solemnly swear (or affirm) that I will support and defend the Constitution of the United States against all enemies, foreign and domestic; that I will bear true faith and allegiance to the same; that I take this obligation freely, without any mental reservation or purpose of evasion; and that I will well and faithfully discharge the duties of the office on which I am about to enter.* The oath ends with the words, *So help me, God.*

The United States Constitution begins with, *We the People.* So then, every citizen of the United States should pledge the oath as found in the first part of the Constitution. Living by an oath was the character of America's Founding Fathers. It was their sacred honor for which they would die that they might preserve their nation.

Americans pledge an oath to the American flag by putting their right hands over their hearts, and reciting the *Pledge of Allegiance. I pledge allegiance to the Flag of the United States of America, and to the Republic for which it stands, one Nation under God, indivisible, with liberty and justice for all.* May we live our lives by dedication, having a purpose.

The second truth epitomizing duty from Psalm 15:4, *to his own hurt*, signifies sacrifice which is something that is offered to God. It is a surrender of one's self. Sometimes we know that we are going to suffer loss for a purpose that is greater than ourselves.

George Washington penned a letter to Congress during the War for Independence asking for provisions. *To see Men without Clothes to cover their nakedness, without Blankets to lay on, without Shoes, by which their Marches might be traced by the Blood from their feet, and almost as often without Provisions as with; Marching through frost and Snow, and at Christmas taking up their Winter Quarters within a day's March of the enemy, without a House or Hut to cover them till they could be built and submitting to it without a murmur, is a mark of patience and obedience which in my opinion can scarce be parallel'd.*

F C YOHN

WINTER AT VALLEY FORGE.
The Relief.

The sacrifice of the American soldier in the Continental Army of the United Colonies during the War for Independence lives on today in the Armed Forces of the United States of America. The call was liberty! The answer was sacrifice! Sacrifice is the price of liberty. Sacrifice called out its challenge, and the American soldier answered the challenge. The American soldier may have been clad in small jackets of white cloth, dirty and ragged, and almost barefoot; but each countenance radiated with the spirit of liberty. The fidelity of duty triumphed for America. This fidelity to duty laid the foundations that America grew upon; those foundations which have sustained America throughout the decades.

Galatians 5:13 *For, brethren, ye have been called unto liberty: only use not liberty for an occasion to the flesh, but by love serve one another.*

Washington Crossing the Delaware
Emanuel Leutze (1851)
Metropolitan Museum of Art, New York City

Philadelphia was in panic, expecting an invasion of Hessian troops hired by King George III. The Continental Congress had fled, leaving instructions: ...*until Congress shall otherwise order, General Washington shall be possessed of full power to order and direct all things.*

General Washington received some information that the Hessians were bivouacked in Trenton, New Jersey just several miles away. The only obstacle was the Delaware River probably easy enough to cross under normal conditions, but Washington and his men were in the middle of a violent, snow storm. There were life-threatening, ice flows in the Delaware River, and Washington was in dire need of clothing, food and ammunition for his men. With the passwords, *Victory or Death*, Washington's troops began to cross the treacherous Delaware River on Christmas Day, December 25, 1776. As they marched toward Trenton, two of Washington's men froze to death. Washington surprised the Hessians early on the morning of December 26, 1776. Alexander Hamilton was firing cannons down the street, and James Monroe, who would be America's fifth President, was wounded in the battle. From that battle the Continental Army received all the food, clothing, and ammunition they needed to continue the fight for liberty. Without their fidelity to duty, America would never have gained independence to become the lighthouse of liberty for the world.

EZRA STILES.

The third aspect of duty is found in the words...*and changeth not*. This signifies determination and resolve. America's Founding Fathers were *doers of the work*. The preachers of the founding era infused a Biblical patriotism into the men of that era; who, in turn, were as the men during Nehemiah's time as stated in Nehemiah 1:17, *They which builded on the wall, and they that bare burdens, with those that laded, every one with one of his hands wrought in the work, and with the other hand held a weapon*. America's Founding Fathers fought with weapons in one hand and built a nation with the other. They had fidelity to their duty and challenged those who wavered in theirs.

Samuel Adams, seeing some men who were vacillating in their resolve to fight, addressed them, *If ye love wealth greater than liberty, the tranquility of servitude greater than the animating contest for freedom, go home from us in peace. We seek not your counsel, nor your arms. Crouch down and lick the hand that feeds you; and may posterity forget that ye were our countrymen.*

These are the times that try men's souls. The summer soldier and the sunshine patriot will, in this crisis, shrink from the service of their country; but he that stands by it now, deserves the love and thanks of man and woman. - Thomas Paine

Samuel Adams

May America always claim that resolve, that fidelity of duty to patriotism so that her citizens may serve their country and be dedicated to serve their Lord and Savior, Jesus Christ.

Ephesians 6:13-17 *Wherefore take unto you the whole armour of God, that ye may be able to withstand in the evil day, and having done all, to stand. Stand therefore, having your loins girt about with truth, and having on the breastplate of righteousness; And your feet shod with the preparation of the gospel of peace; Above all, taking the shield of faith, wherewith ye shall be able to quench all the fiery darts of the wicked And take the helmet of salvation, and the sword of the Spirit, which is the word of God:*

America is coming into some trying times again, and she must learn from those who have proceeded her. American citizens must have that determination, a resolve to guard their nation and to realize that, *We the People* means they have a Biblical responsibility; a duty to their nation.

John Quincy Adams

These three aspects of oath, sacrifice, and resolve equal the fidelity of duty. John Quincy Adams said, *Duty is ours, results are God's.*

The liberties of our country, the freedoms of our civil Constitution are worth defending at all hazards; it is our duty to defend them against all attacks. We have received them as a fair inheritance from our worthy ancestors. They purchased them for us with toil and danger and expense of treasure and blood. It will bring a mark of everlasting infamy on the present generation – enlightened as it is – if we should suffer them to be wrested from us by violence without a struggle, or to be cheated out of them by the artifices of designing men. - Samuel Adams

The man who is conscientiously doing his duty will ever be protected by that righteous and all-powerful Being; and when he has finished his work, he will receive an ample reward. - Samuel Adams

John Hancock

While we are using the means in our power, let us humbly commit our righteous cause to the great Lord of the Universe, who loveth righteousness and hateth iniquity. And having secured the approbation of our hearts, by a faithful and unwearied discharge of our duty to our country, let us joyfully leave our concerns in the hands of him who raiseth up and pulleth down the empires and kingdoms of the world as he pleases; and with cheerful submission to his sovereign will. - John Hancock

John Jay

John Jay, the original Chief Justice of the Supreme Court, President of Congress, and one of the authors of the *Federalist Papers* who is considered one of the three men most responsible for us having the Constitution today was a strong Christian. He stated that, *All that the best men can do is to persevere in doing their duty to their country and leave the consequences to Him who made it their duty, being neither elated by success, however great, nor discouraged by disappointment, however frequent and mortifying.*

Abraham Clark

Abraham Clark, a signer of the Declaration of Independence, had two sons captured by the British and was told that they would be remanded to a *Prisoner of War* ship. This was a death penalty with a slow agonizing death in the belly of a ship. If he recanted, he would have his sons returned to him. Even with their lives at stake, he would not agree.

Even though America's Founding Fathers were willing to give their all, no matter the cost, they made a pledge to each other to do their duty. *With firm reliance upon divine protection we pledge to each other our lives, our fortunes and our sacred honor.* Americans, too, must pledge to do their duty, no matter the cost. God and country need men and women, young and old to ask themselves the question, *Where is my place? What is my duty? Am I doing it?*

Romans 14:7 *For none of us liveth to himself, and no man dieth to himself.*

Benjamin Rush

Benjamin Rush, referring to this verse said, *But remember that none of us liveth to himself. Even our old age is not our own property. All its fruits of wisdom and experience belong to the public. To do good is the business of life. To enjoy rest is the happiness of heaven.*

Americans must live their lives for others, for their children, for future generations and the continuance of the United States of America.

Robert Morris

Robert Morris was chosen as the financier of the War for Independence. In order to keep the government running, he issued $1.4 million of "Morris notes" backed by his own credit and borrowed substantial amounts from his business acquaintances. He took great financial risks in order to fund the Yorktown Campaign that ended in Gen. Charles Cornwallis' defeat. America could not repay him because there was no money; and yet, Robert Morris never complained because he had given his word. In the later years of his life, he spent four years in debtor's prison.

Surrender of Lord Cornwallis at Yorktown

Why was Robert Morris willing to give it all? It was for a cause bigger than himself. It was for the future of America. He was sacrificing for future generations.

Andre Malaux wrote, *Civilizations come into being only when they strive for the kind of man who believes he has more duties than rights.*

In America's current culture many want nothing to do with duty. They want all the rights but none of the duties. This type of attitude leads to servitude. They do not understand for every right, there is a duty to perform. America has had it so good for so long that the meaning of duty has been greatly diminished. Most Americans have not had to do their duty on foreign battle fields. Only ten percent of World War II veterans are still alive today. Many do not consider the reason why America is so unique in her design and such a wonder of the world in her liberty and prosperity. The reason is that Americans have always possessed an exceptional understanding of and a commitment to the concept of duty.

George Washington wrote, *The consideration that human happiness and moral duty are inseparably connected will always continue to prompt me to promote the progress of the former by inculcating the practice of the latter.*

While we are zealously performing the duties of good citizens and soldiers, we certainly ought not to be inattentive to the higher duties of religion. To the distinguished character of Patriot, it should be our highest glory to add the more distinguished character of Christian. [SOURCE: George Washington, *General Orders* (2 May 1778); published in *Writings of George Washington* (1932), Vol.XI, pp. 342-343]

In such a state of things it is in an especial manner our duty as a people, with devout reverence and affectionate gratitude, to acknowledge our many and great obligations to Almighty God and to implore Him to continue and confirm the blessings we experience. Deeply penetrated with this sentiment, I, George Washington, President of the United States, do recommend to all religious societies and denominations, and to all persons whomsoever, within the United States to set apart and observe Thursday, the 19th day of February next as a day of public thanksgiving and prayer, and on that day to meet together and render their sincere and hearty thanks to the Great Ruler of Nations for the manifold and signal mercies which distinguish our lot as a nation... It is to be noted that there is genuine piety expressed in this statement..., [SOURCE: *In A Life of Washington* (1836) by James K. Paulding, *Washington's Thanksgiving Proclamation*]

How do Americans live by oaths of dedication, by living sacrificial lives, by having the resolve they need to do their duty to God and to their government?

Hebrews 12:2 *Looking unto Jesus the author and finisher of our faith; who for the joy that was set before him endured the cross, despising the shame, and is set down at the right hand of the throne of God.*

The USS *Samuel Chase* disembarks troops of Company E, 16th Infantry, 1st Infantry Division onto the Fox Green section of Omaha Beach in Normandy, France on the morning of June 6, 1944.

I had the opportunity to go to Normandy, France several years ago. When I accepted the invitation, I did not know I would be going with a veteran from the D-Day invasion who helped to liberate that portion of France from the tyrannical grasp of Nazi Germany. On the flight over, we sat for seven hours through the night talking. The World War II veteran was eighty-four years old at the time. I asked him, after some time had passed, if he would like to get some sleep, but he replied that he felt fine and asked if I had any more questions. Of course, I did. I was sitting beside living history. When we arrived in Normandy, we stood on a section of beach the Allied Forces had termed *Omaha* when I asked Bill what it was like when he had landed all those years ago. Bill paused, and I could see his keen mind going back to that day in World War II when he was in the 3rd Special-Armored division. Bill told me he was not sure if he landed D-Day plus one or two because he had been waiting in a landing craft for hours.

He stood there on that sandy beach as waves gently encroached upon our position, and he looked out into the water. Bill told me that during the D-Day invasion as far as the eye could see there were ships and boats of every size and description. Looking up, at times, the sky was seemingly dark with aircraft bringing in men and munitions. When his unit reached the shoreline there were bodies of American men laying all over the beach and floating in the water. Some of the men were moaning; they were still alive. All had been faithful to do their duty to that last good measure.

Later that day, we were eating in a typical French cafe by the beach. There were several at the table, and Bill was noticeably older than the rest of the men sitting there. We were enjoying the meal and the conversation when I noticed a French woman seated within earshot of our table listening to our conversation. She was an older woman with graying hair but refined in her mannerisms. When she had finished her plate of mussels, she approached our table and apologized for interrupting our meal. She looked at Bill and asked, *Were you one of the men who landed here during the D-Day invasion?*

Bill answered, *Yes, I was.*

I looked at the French woman who was beginning to tear up. Her next question was, *How old were you?*

Bill replied, *I was eighteen years old.*

Now the French woman began to openly weep. Through sobs she told Bill, *Thank you for risking your life to save mine. If you had not been willing to do what you did, I would have grown up a slave to Nazisism.*

Bill looked at the woman and smiled. Very humbly he said, *Thank you, Madame, but you see I was just doing my duty.*

May all Americans humbly find what their duty is to the United States of America and perform it with the same fidelity of purpose and to the best of their several abilities as those who have preceded them.

The Normandy American Cemetery

Whate'er thy race or speech, thou art the same;
Before thy eyes Duty, a constant flame,
Shines always steadfast with unchanging light,
Through dark days and through bright.

The Ode of Life

Chapter Seven

Foundations of Freedom

If the foundations be destroyed, what can the righteous do? This question is asked in the Holy Bible in Psalm 11:3. The word, *foundations*, comes from a Hebrew word meaning *the settled order of things*. In this verse, David likened *the settled order of things* in society to a building. This building of society is built upon the foundations of law and order along with justice and truth. These are the very qualities upon which civilizations are built.

Calvin Coolidge

President Calvin Coolidge said on October 15, 1924, *There are only two theories of government in the world. One rests in righteousness, the other on force. One appeals to reason, the other appeals to the sword. One is exemplified in a republic, the other is represented by despotism.*

Saul Threatening David by José Leonardo

The eroding foundations of the Hebrew government in David's day have some striking similarities to the eroding foundations in American government today. This erosion has accelerated over the last five decades. David had a front row seat in which to witness the corruption of the court of King Saul. The very things Saul was supposed to protect, those were the things he was eroding, was minimizing, and was dismantling. Too many times the old adage is true, *The one thing we learn from history is that we don't learn from history*. If a nation does not learn from the past, that nation is bound to repeat the mistakes from the past that have already been made.

America's Founding Fathers formulated a national birth-certificate unlike any other on earth; hence, the United States of America is the longest on-going constitutional republic in the history of the world. All national governments have changed since the inception of the United States, and few, if any, have enjoyed the stability and prosperity Americans have experienced under the Declaration of Independence and the United States Constitution. There must be a remembrance by Americans that the blessings they share are not by chance. These blessing in America should never cause any sense of American superiority for America's blessings must be recognized for what they are; blessings from God.

Up to the time of the founding of America, most of the governments in the world were monarchies; governments of men which said that rights and freedoms from God were given to the king, and then the king would give these rights and freedoms, as he wished, to the people. This meant one's life and liberty were dependent upon the king's benevolence or, on the other hand, one's life and liberty were subjected to the king's malevolence when he took that one's rights and freedoms away.

America's Founding Fathers, fifty-six men, stood up out of the humdrum of history and said, *Wrong*. These men were students of the Holy Bible. They said that freedom and rights came from God, not from kings, and went directly to the people who then would entrust those freedoms and rights to the government, as the people saw fit, so that government could disperse those rights and freedoms by the consent of the governed. They said, *God grants us our rights not the Constitution and to secure these rights, governments are instituted among men deriving their just powers from the consent of the governed*. This meant the American government would not be able to do anything without the permission of the people, and these people would then be tempered by the United States Constitution which would be America's supreme, rule of law.

Prophet Samuel

In the ancient days of Israel, the Prophet Samuel warned Israel about the type of man a king would become if he wielded absolute power. In 1 Samuel 8:11-17, Samuel uses the phrase *he will take* six times. The result is found in verse eighteen. *And ye shall cry out in that day because of your king which ye shall have chosen you; and the Lord will not hear you in that day.* The people's response is given in the next verse. *Nevertheless the people refused to obey the voice of Samuel; and they said, Nay; but we will have a king over us.* **That we also may be like all the nations***; and that our king may judge us, and go out before us, and fight our battles.*

It is interesting to see in world history that America's Founding Fathers were Biblically based when they made a declaration to the rest of the world that they represented Americans who did not wish to be like all the other nations. The signers of the Declaration of Independence declared they did not want a king to reign over them any longer. These men were counting on God to fight for them. Anyone reviewing the American War for Independence can see how many times God miraculously intervened for the outnumbered patriots. The motto of the War for Independence was *No King, but King Jesus,* and the seal was *Rebellion to Tyrants Is Obedience to God*.

America's Founding Fathers sought liberty not license; not a loosening of restraints but freedom to do what was right. Their objective was the safety and happiness of their fellow citizens; in other words, a common defense, a general welfare, or the blessings of liberty. Some may envision these men as rash and rowdy rebels, but that was not the case for they were already accomplished in their fields of endeavor and were men settled in character and reputation. They could have led lives of ease and comfort had they been willing to bow to the king of England, but they would not. They chose liberty over luxury. They were men of purpose and principle who well understood the peril of choosing to declare independence from Great Britain.

George Whitfield Preaching During the Great Awakening

These founders were men who grew up in the Great Awakening. Many were profoundly influenced by the preachers of the day who spoke not from beautifully carved pulpits but from the stumps of old trees; not from church facilities but, many times, in the open air. They declared obtaining eternal life was not conformation to a State-run church but through a personal relationship with the Savior, the LORD Jesus Christ. Fire and passion of righteousness were the common threads which permeated each pulpit and which ignited a fire within many of the American Founding Fathers' hearts; burning so brightly it spread to many others.

Dr. Benjamin Rush

John Adams

Dr. Benjamin Rush said to John Adams, *Do you recollect the pensive and awful silence which pervaded the House when we were called up, one after another, to the table by the President of Congress to subscribe to what was believed by many at that time to be our death warrants?*

How could they endure so much? It was because the cause for liberty meant so much. Today it has been said, *Freedom is not free.*

John Quincy Adams

These were men of great vision and deep spiritual conviction. Knowing it was God who gave American patriots strength and power to win the War for Independence was cause for appreciation and humility on the birthday of the United States.

On July 4, 1837, some sixty-one years after the Declaration of Independence, President John Quincy Adams delivered an oration in which he noted America's two most popular holidays (Christmas and the Fourth of July) were inseparably intertwined: *In the chain of human events, the birthday of the nation is indissolubly linked with the birthday of the Savior. It forms a leading event in the progress of the Gospel dispensation. The Declaration of Independence first organized the social compact on the foundation of the Redeemer's mission on earth [and] laid the cornerstone of human government on the first precepts of Christianity.*

American freedom has come under attack in years past with World War I, World War II, the Korean War, the Vietnam War, Desert Storm, and currently the war in Afghanistan and Iraq. Today the followers of violent, extremist ideologies are patiently plotting to destroy America's entire culture. In every generation, the world has produced enemies of freedom. They have attacked America because America is freedom's home and has been its defender. America has always been the land of the free because she is the home of the brave.

Arnold Toynbee

There is a more insidious attack upon America that has been waging since the 1940s. This attack is from within, and it is leveled at the very foundations of America's freedoms. It is an attack upon the foundations of the home, of the family, of the churches, of the government, of the educational institutions, of the economy, and of the free-market system. These foundations of freedom make up the national identity of America and unless the enemies of these freedoms are defeated, their insidious attack will adversely affect the future of the United States of America. Arnold Toynbee, a famous world historian, pointed to the fact that almost all great civilizations have not been overthrown by some outside aggressor but by moral and spiritual collapse on the inside.

Alexander Tyler

Alexander Tyler in 1760 said that world history teaches us the average age of the world's great civilizations have been around 200 years. These nations have progressed through the following sequence: *From bondage to spiritual faith; from spiritual faith to courage; from courage to liberty; from liberty to abundance; from abundance to selfishness; from selfishness to complacency; from complacency to apathy; from apathy to dependency; from dependence back again to bondage.* Where is America? It is in the dependency stage, just one step away from being back in bondage. Industries and jobs are moving south of the border and overseas due to unfair trade practices with foreign nations. Many of the products in America are now *Made in China*. Over sixty percent of the oil America imports is from middle-eastern countries that want the demise of the United States of America. At one time America was admired by the community of nations, but now America is a by-word. The United States of America is still the leading country in many good things, but sadly she is leading with other countries in numerous wrong things, such as: violent crime, divorce, teen pregnancies, abortions, drug abuse, illiteracy, and pornography.

General Douglas MacArthur

The Bible says in Proverbs 14:34, *Righteousness exalteth a nation: but sin is a reproach to any people.* God says in Psalm 9:17, *The wicked shall be turned into hell, and all the nations that forget God.* The Bible says in Job 12:23, *He increaseth the nations, and destroyeth them: he enlargeth the nations, and straiteneth them again.* More than a century after the founding of the United States, General Douglas MacArthur insisted, *History fails to record a single precedent, in which nations subject to moral decay, have not passed into political and economic decline. There has been either a spiritual awakening to overcome the moral lapse or a progressive deterioration leading to ultimate national disaster.*

President John Adams observed, *It must be felt that there is no national security but in the nation's humble acknowledged dependence upon God and his overruling providence.*

WENDELL PHILLIPS

Etched in granite in Washington, D.C. are the words, *Eternal vigilance is the price of liberty*, attributed to Wendell Phillips, 1811-1884; who was an abolitionist, orator and columnist for the *Liberator* and who gave these words in a speech before the Massachusetts Anti-Slavery Society in 1852 according to the *Dictionary of Quotations* edited by Bergen Evans. Most Americans have not been vigilant. They have been enjoying the peace and the prosperity liberty brings but not guarding the liberty itself. It is time for Americans to wake up.

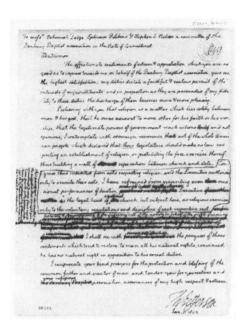

Thomas Jefferson's Letter to the Danbury Baptists

Many Christian Americans have fallen under the lie concerning the separation of church and state. President Thomas Jefferson in an address to the Danbury Baptists on January 1, 1802 states that the First Amendment has built *a wall of separation between Church & State:*

Letter to the Danbury Baptists
January 1, 1802

To messers. Nehemiah Dodge, Ephraim Robbins, & Stephen S. Nelson, a committee of the Danbury Baptist association in the state of Connecticut

Gentlemen

The affectionate sentiments of esteem and approbation which you are so good as to express towards me, on behalf of the Danbury Baptist association, give me the highest satisfaction. My duties dictate a faithful and zealous pursuit of the interests of my constituents, & in proportion as they are persuaded of my fidelity to those duties, the discharge of them becomes more and more pleasing.

Believing with you that religion is a matter which lies solely between Man &
his God, that he owes account to none other for his faith or his worship, that the
legitimate powers of government reach actions only, & not opinions, I contemplate
with sovereign reverence that act of the whole American people which declared
that their legislature should "make no law respecting an establishment of religion,
or prohibiting the free exercise thereof," thus building a wall of separation between
Church & State. Adhering to this expression of the supreme will of the nation in
behalf of the rights of conscience, I shall see with sincere satisfaction the progress
of those sentiments which tend to restore to man all his natural rights, convinced
he has no natural right in opposition to his social duties.

I reciprocate your kind prayers for the protection & blessing of the common father
and creator of man, and tender you for yourselves & your religious association,
assurances of my high respect & esteem.

Th. Jefferson

This letter clearly states there is a one directional wall; that wall keeps
the government from interfering with the church. This letter also
makes it clear that individuals in America, though religious, have no
natural right to be in opposition to his or her social duties. In Jefferson's
words, *I shall see with sincere satisfaction the progress of those sentiments which*
tend to restore to man all his natural rights, convinced he has no natural right
in opposition to his social duties. All American citizens have a duty to be
involved in all things which better American society which includes the
American citizen's government.

If we lose a recognition of God's hand in our culture, and God's hand in our
nation. If we lose the idea that we have a dependence upon Him there is no way
our nation will last. - George Washington.

When God is absent, sin and evil are present. When absolutes are
removed from society or when you say to others they can do whatever
they want, the dramatic results will be an increase in violent crimes, in
immorality, and in vice. Where is America heading? What realization
does America need? What resolutions must America have?

Citizens Voting, 1944

Many tremendous changes can be accomplished when the political process is understood, when a working knowledge of the Constitution is obtained, and when the duty of the citizen is once again fulfilled. One of the most basic responsibilities of the citizen is to cast an informed vote in every election. Of course all of these principles are energized when bathed in prayer by asking God to bless the endeavors of the leadership of America and by asking God to bless the endeavors of every citizen who desires to maintain America's liberty.

2 Chronicles 7:14 *If my people, which are called by my name, shall humble themselves, and pray, and seek my face, and turn from their wicked ways; then will I hear from heaven, and will forgive their sin, and will heal their land.*

There is an exhortation in the Holy Bible to supplicate, to pray, to intercede, and to give thanks for those in government. First Timothy 2:1-5 states, *I exhort therefore, that, first of all, supplications, prayers, intercessions, and giving of thanks, be made for all men; For kings, and for all that are in authority; that we may lead a quiet and peaceable life in all godliness and honesty. For this is good and acceptable in the sight of God our Saviour; Who will have all men to be saved, and to come unto the knowledge of the truth. For there is one God, and one mediator between God and men, the man Christ Jesus;*

It is the responsibility of every American citizen to take a leadership role in fortifying America's foundations upon which she was built. God's providential protection, presence, power, purposes, and principles are the footings of the foundation of America. These footings can be and should be strengthened by all America citizens who love their nation.

Buildings in Washington, D.C. Under Construction

National Archives

The Capitol

Washington Monument

Lincoln Memorial

Jefferson Memorial

Psalm 11:3 *If the foundations be destroyed, what can the righteous do?*

Chapter Eight

Foundations of American Fabric

To many the American Ideal of *E Pluribus Unum* is unknown in meaning and history, yet when an American citizen learns its meaning and its origin, that citizen has a lasting impression as well as a thought-provoking understanding of the multicultural fabric of his or her great nation. What is the meaning of this American Ideal? Where did this American Ideal originate?

Immigrants Landing at Castle Garden

America's history reveals that the Castle Garden office in the southwest tip of Battery Park, New York was America's first, immigrant center. The doors of this immigration office opened in 1855 and had more than 8 million immigrants pass through them before they closed on April 18, 1890. Before the opening of this first immigration office, immigrants coming into New York Harbor would just appear at public docks and then melt into American society with no record of their entrance; hence, the Castle Garden office opened to become the first orderly way in which to handle immigrants entering America.

Interior View of the Office at Castle Garden

Castle Garden and Liberty Island

The *Statue of Liberty* was built on Liberty Island in New York Harbor. Any immigrants coming into the harbor going to the immigration center would be greeted by her. The *Statue of Liberty's* construction began in the 1870s, and its dedication was on October 28, 1886. The designer of this American symbol of freedom was Frederic Auguste Bartholdi, and the builder was Gustave Eiffel. The *Statue of Liberty* was a beautiful gift to the United States from the people of France and became a welcomed sight to the immigrants entering America who hoped to become a part of the American, national fabric.

The Battery Outside of the Barge Office

On April 19, 1890, the Castle Garden immigration center moved to a temporary, barge office on the southeast tip of Battery Park, New York while a new, immigration-center complex was being constructed on Ellis Island in New York Harbor. An island was chosen for this office to ensure immigrants disembarking in America would not just melt into American society unnoticed. Before the complex on Ellis Island was completed, nearly a quarter of a million immigrants passed through the temporary, barge office until its closing on December 31, 1891. Though this temporary office had been closed, it would be used again briefly after a fire caused great damage to the Ellis Island complex.

First Immigrant Station at Ellis Island

Statue of Annie Moore and Her Brothers
Photo by: Peter Craine

The Saint Daily Globe
January 02, 1892

p. 2

No More Barge Office
Immigrants will here after land at Ellis Island

New York, Jan 1. Without any ceremony or formal opening the immigration officials of this city today settled down on Ellis Island in the harbor and the barge office is known to them no more. The steamship Nevada was the first to arrive at the new landing place. Her immigrants were put aboard the barge J.E. Moore, and amid the blowing of fog horns and whistles approached the pier. Charles M. Hanley, private secretary to the late Secretary Windom, who had asked permission to be allowed to register the first immigrant, was at the registry deck when there came tripping up fifteen-year-old Annie Moore and her little brother. They came from Cork to meet their mother, who lives here. Col. Weber greeted Annie and...presented her with a crisp new $10 bill.

As fifteen-year-old Annie Moore approached Ellis Island on January 1, 1892, she would be the first immigrant to walk through the doors of the new complex on Ellis Island constructed for the purpose of assimilating immigrants into the United States of America. Annie and her two brothers, Anthony and Philip, were travelling from County Cork, Ireland to join their parents who were already in America. Arriving on Ellis Island, Annie and her brothers entered the new building and headed for a medical evaluation, then finished their registration, answered an interview, and finally hurried down a flight of stairs to their waiting relatives. On that special day Annie, being the first to go through the new building, was registered and then given ten dollars. Some say it was a crisp ten-dollar bill; the majority stating Annie was given a ten-dollar, Liberty gold-piece. Depending on the year of the gold-piece, Annie would have seen the Great America Seal with *E Pluribus Unum* imprinted on a banner held by a great eagle, or she would have seen *In God We Trust* engraved on a banner above the head of a great eagle. This gift was a wonderful keepsake for this young lady who had travelled so far to begin a new life alongside so many differing people in America yet had been content to become one with them in liberty.

Leaving the magnificent building Annie would have walked out the doors to once again see the *Statue of Liberty* on Liberty Island confirming the welcome she had felt upon entering New York Harbor. No matter the details of January 1, 1892, Annie Moore and her two brothers personify the embodiment of *E Pluribus Unum* in action by beginning their quest for American citizenship.

America's Founding Fathers desired the phrase, *E Pluribus Unum*, to be apparent to every American citizen. These founders agreed *E Pluribus Unum* was likened unto an artist taking various colors and blending them onto a canvas; making many diverse hues into one, beautiful portrait. This portrait very well illustrates the fabric of society in the United States of America. *E Pluribus Unum* then depicts the American Ideal.

This expression, *E Pluribus Unum*, was the basis for the creation of the Great Seal of America. John Adams, Benjamin Franklin and Thomas Jefferson on July 4, 1776 were given the task of creating a seal that would define America, and six years later after dismissing several ideas for other seals, these Founding Fathers chose the Great American Seal of the *eagle*. In the eagle's beak is a ribbon with the Latin words, *E Pluribus Unum*, with one of its talons holding an olive branch depicting peace and with the other talon, it is holding a bundle of arrows illustrating the power of war. On the eagle's breast is a shield with thirteen red and white stripes which stands for the first, thirteen colonies in America while a cloud above the eagle with thirteen stars represents a new nation among many nations. These Founding Fathers selected the Latin phrase, *E Pluribus Unum*, by reasoning it best portrayed the unification of diverse immigrants living within America's first, thirteen colonies into one nation. They adopted this American Ideal because the literal translation is *from several one or out of many one*. Still the question remains. Where did *E Pluribus Unum* originate? Many have asked this question and over the life of the United States of America, many have searched for the answer.

The Evening Times
Grand Forks, ND
February 14, 1911

p. 47

Origin of "E Pluribus Unum"
Near Phrase Appears in Many Old Manuscripts, Notably In a Latin Poem

This is the season when the American nation is passing through its meteoric shower of natal anniversaries. The birthdays of Washington, Jefferson, Lincoln, Grant and other famous men are being celebrated. It may, therefore, be seasonable to inquire whence came the motto of the United States, "E Pluribus Unum." The merest tyro in Latin can translate, one from many; a union now of forty-six, soon to be forty-eight, states. But where did the revolutionary patriots, who had it inscribed upon the great seal of the United States of America, find the perfectly fitting phrase? Of course, it cannot be regarded as a momentous mystery, but for a century many people who have been seeking origins have been baffled in their quest.

Some time in the winter of 1879-80 I remember James A. Garfield, then a member of the house, and the newly fledged Senator Hoar came rushing into the library of congress and confronted A.R. Spofford, the custodian of its books. Three more classical cranks could not have been assembled to brew a caldron of pure pedantry with which to stimulate at times their practical legislation. The question which had caused the foregathering was precisely this one of where was the fountain head of "E Pluribus Unum." The next day curiosity emboldened me to ask Mr. Garfield how the ransacking of the authorities had resulted. Nothing plausible could be found except that on the title page of the Gentleman's magazine, from 1731 to 1901, a London periodical, this exact Latin phrase had always been printed as its motto.

E Pluribus Unum

The words run across a bouquet of flowers, and striking patness is shown by the added explanation, "collected chiefly from public papers by Sylvanius Urban." Off the stage Sylvanius Urban was Edward Cave, a noted figure in English politics and letters.

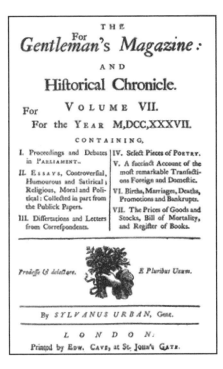

THE
For
Gentleman's Magazine:

A N D

Hiſtorical Chronicle.

For   V O L U M E VII.

For the Y E A R M,DCC,XXXVII.

CONTAINING,

I. Proceedings and Debates in PARLIAMENT.
II. ESSAYS, Controverſial, Humourous and Satirical; Religious, Moral and Political: Collected in part from the Publick Papers.
III. Diſſertations and Letters from Correſpondents.

IV. Select Pieces of POETRY.
V. A ſuccinct Account of the moſt remarkable Tranſactions Foreign and Domeſtic.
VI. Births, Marriages, Deaths, Promotions and Bankrupts.
VII. The Prices of Goods and Stocks, Bill of Mortality, and Regiſter of Books.

Prodeſſe & delectare.   *E Pluribus Unum.*

By *SYLVANUS URBAN,* Gent.

L O N D O N:
Printed by EDW. CAVE, at St. JOHN's GATE.

Of course, there was exhibited the precise phrase, and this magazine was regularly appearing during the sixteen years the device of the American seal was under incubation. But it was not a classical origin, and Mr. Garfield was not satisfied. It only removed the question further back—where did Cave find his magazine motto? That remains an enigms, and so does the exact source of the "E Pluribus Unum" motto on the seal. Statesmen of that day grabbled in their diaries like barbers about every trivial topic, but none tells about the motto. Apparently until 1893, when the government made its exhibit at the world's fair, our familiar friend, the "consensus of opinion," rested content with ascribing the origin to the English magazine. A facsimile of the national seal was shown at the fair and an official of the state department prepared a valuable monograph upon the adoption of its design in 1782.

The history of the seal is now quite well authenticated in all its details, but these annals also lamentably fail to disclose whence came the motto. However, a new quest began and now it is possible to find in a few reference books the claim that "E Pluribus Unum" is to be found in a poem by Virgil, called "Morotum" (a salad.) The original quotation in Latin reads:

It manus in gyrum, paullatim singula vires
Deperdunt propias, color est e pluribus unus.

Depiction of Virgil, 3rd Century A.D.

This poem of "Morotum" is but 125 lines in length and the line containing the assumed origin of the motto is the one hundred and third. The youthful skit by the writer of the "Aeneid" tells about a farmer going out into his garden to gather the ingredients of a salad. The herbs are culled and brought in, where the oil is ready and then, freely translating the Latin quoted: He grinds them in the mortar, gradually each vegetable hue and there is one color from many.

Now, the careful reader of the Latin couplet will note that the phrase is "E pluribus unus" and not "unum." It will not be too "classical" to explain that Virgil had to write "unus" and "unum" for, as an adjective, it had to agree in gender with "color," which is masculine. Hence it will not do for certain careless authors of "quotation" books to change the accurate text and make it read "E pluribus unum." Therefore, the exact American motto has not yet been traced to any classical source. In one of Horace's "Epistles" there occurs the phrase, "De pluribus una," when he is alluding to the drawing out of a thorn. St. Augustine, in his "confessions," comes pretty close to the required phrase, for he writes, "Expluribus unum facore" (to make one from many.)

It is just this question of gender that ruins the whole hunt. It will not do to sneer at gender just because the Romans had some peculiar rules governing it, for American children are taught grammar, and good writers must observe English usage above the gender of nouns and pronouns. Therefore, does not the new query obtrude: What was the thing of neuter gender to which the congress of 1782 wanted "E pluribus unum" to apply? Such words as nation, republic, union, etc. are all feminine, at least not neuter. It certainly does seem that if Mr. Jefferson be the real suggester of the American motto he was nodding over his Latin gender.

It is not necessary to prolong this search and recount the manner in which the seal was adopted. On the very afternoon of the day that independence was declared Franklin, Adams and Jefferson were made a committee to report a design for a seal. Each did report some elaborate devices depicting scenes from Holy Writ, the landing of Hengist and Hersa, the leaders of the Jutes, in England, and even some choice selections from the legend of Hercules. Each of these eminent patriots had his own selection of mottoes. Finally Jefferson was appointed to report a composite design of the separate reports and upon his first appears "E pluribus unum." It does not matter if sixteen years later a design by William Barton of Philadelphia was adopted, for he took the Jefferson motto as it stands today.

Ben Franklin

John Adams

Thomas Jefferson

It would seem, therefore, that the Gentleman's magazine title page did furnish the motto. The famous publisher, Edward Cave, died long before the revolution. He had been a great friend of Ben Franklin and used his lightning rods upon his splendid London mansion. The magazine must have had large circulation in the colonies. Perhaps Cave appropriated his motto from Virgil and changed the gender to make it neuter, as it must be in English, but this is clumsy work. It obviously results in "hog Latin."

But one item more. It is known that Virgil had a Greek tutor named Pharnetius and he wrote in Greek a poem about making a salad, and it is also said that Virgil's poem is but an imitation of the Greek original. Perhaps, then, our American motto may have a Hellenic fountain. All that Pharnetius wrote has perished, except a score of erotic tales similar to "Boccacio's Decameron." —
Pittsburg Dispatch

Many Americans, as they view the early immigrants entering New York Harbor, must remember these were they who came before to build a heritage of privilege for future Americans to enjoy; one American generation giving birth to another. These immigrants of America came with just a few keepsakes or maybe even just the clothes on their back, tired from their travels; yet elated by the freedom America afforded them. Though diverse these immigrants looked to *E Pluribus Unum* to open the way of opportunity for them to become an American citizen. You see, America is a beautiful bouquet of many different flowers; from many gardens these flowers have become one. As I write this chapter, I am a grateful American whose ancestors along with my wife's ancestors dreamed, struggled, and clawed to become citizens of the United States of America. We did not come to America to create little factions, who live by other countries' standards. We are Americans. We came to become American citizens who chose to live by the laws and statutes of freedom birthed in America; the Declaration of Independence and the Constitution of the United States of America.

Rebuilt Immigrant Station on Ellis Island

For over 200 years, eager immigrants have flowed into America. To become an American citizen, each has raised his or her right hand and has repeated an Oath of Allegiance; this Oath of Allegiance emphasizing several promises. What is this Oath of Allegiance?

The principles embodied in the Oath of Allegiance are codified in Section 337(a) in the Immigration and Nationality Act (INA), which provides that all applicants shall take an oath that incorporates the substance of the following:

1.Support the Constitution;
2.Renounce and abjure absolutely and entirely all allegiance and fidelity to any foreign prince, potentate, state, or sovereignty of whom or which the applicant was before a subject or citizen;
3.Support and defend the Constitution and laws of the United States against all enemies, foreign and domestic;
4.Bear true faith and allegiance to the same; and
5.A. Bear arms on behalf of the United States when required by the law; or
6.B. Perform noncombatant service in the Armed Forces of the United States when required by the law; or
7.C. Perform work of national importance under civilian direction when required by the law.

The language of the current Oath is found in the Code of Federal Regulations Section 337.1 and is closely based upon the statutory elements in Section 337(a) of the INA.

The U.S. Citizenship and Immigration Service also shares a brief history of the Oath of Allegiance in its beginning days in the year 1790 up to 1929, stating that an applicant, *"...shall...declare, on oath...that he will support the Constitution of the United States, and that he absolutely and entirely renounces and abjures all allegiance and fidelity to every foreign prince, potentate, state, or sovereignty; and, particularly, by name, to the prince, potentate, state, or sovereignty of which he was before a citizen or subject; which proceedings shall be recorded by the clerk of the court."*

With time the process has grown in order and decorum:

An official standard text for the Oath of Allegiance did not appear in the regulations until 1929. The regulation said that before a naturalization certificate could be issued, the applicant should take the following oath in court:

I hereby declare, on oath, that I absolutely and entirely renounce and abjure all allegiance and fidelity to any foreign prince, potentate, State, or sovereignty, and particularly to _____ of who (which) I have heretofore been a subject (or citizen); that I will support and defend the Constitution and laws of the United States of America against all enemies, foreign and domestic; that I will bear true faith and allegiance to the same; and that I take this obligation freely without any mental reservation or purpose of evasion: So help me God. In acknowledgment whereof I have hereunto affixed my signature.

Until today where the Oath of Allegiance states:

I hereby declare, on oath, that I absolutely and entirely renounce and abjure all allegiance and fidelity to any foreign prince, potentate, state, or sovereignty, of whom or which I have heretofore been a subject or citizen; that I will support and defend the Constitution and laws of the United States of America against all enemies, foreign and domestic; that I will bear true faith and allegiance to the same; that I will bear arms on behalf of the United States when required by the law; that I will perform noncombatant service in the Armed Forces of the United States when required by the law; that I will perform work of national importance under civilian direction when required by the law; and that I take this obligation freely, without any mental reservation or purpose of evasion; so help me God."

(https://www.uscis.gov/us-citizenship)

As I have examined the process of citizenship with an understanding of *E Pluribus Unum*, I have realized American citizenship is a privilege Americans must cherish. There is one more question still we must address. What does it take to lose one's honor of American citizenship or naturalization? Many American citizens have never pondered this question; yet the answer is very clear as you read the laws established.

(The SOURCE for the following laws is
https://www.uscis.gov/us-citizenship)

In general, a person is subject to revocation of naturalization on the following grounds:

A. Person Procures Naturalization Illegally

A person is subject to revocation of naturalization if he or she procured naturalization illegally. Procuring naturalization illegally simply means that the person was not eligible for naturalization in the first place...

B. Concealment of Material Fact or Willful Misrepresentation

...

1. Concealment of Material Fact or Willful Misrepresentation

A person is subject to revocation of naturalization if there is deliberate deceit on the part of the person in misrepresenting or failing to disclose a material fact or facts on his or her naturalization application and subsequent examination...

2. Membership or Affiliation with Certain Organizations

A person is subject to revocation of naturalization if the person becomes a member of, or affiliated with, the Communist party, other totalitarian party, or terrorist organization within five years of his or her naturalization...In general, a person who is involved with such organizations cannot establish the naturalization requirements of having an attachment to the Constitution and of being well-disposed to the good order and happiness of the United States...

The fact that a person becomes involved with such an organization within five years after the date of naturalization is prima facie evidence that he or she concealed or willfully misrepresented material evidence that would have prevented the person's naturalization.

C. Other than Honorable Discharge before Five Years of Honorable Service after Naturalization

Summary

American citizens are privileged people. Is it any wonder individuals spend the last, little bit of strength and fortune to come to the United States of America? Americans must stop often and consider where God has allowed them to live and to rear their families. America's Founding Fathers understood that the fabric of the United States of America would be one of *E Pluribus Unum*. They penned the following words in the Declaration of Independence:

*We hold these truths to be self-evident, that **all men are created equal**, that they are endowed by their Creator with certain unalienable Rights, that among these are Life, Liberty and the pursuit of Happiness.*

Chapter Nine

Foundations of Forgiveness

How Firm a Foundation
FOUNDATION

"K" — in Rippon's *Selection of Hymns*, 1787

American melody
From Caldwell's *Union Harmony*, 1837

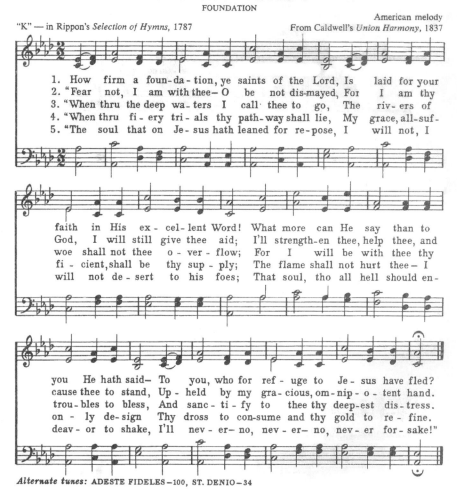

1. How firm a foun-da-tion, ye saints of the Lord, Is laid for your
2. "Fear not, I am with thee— O be not dis-mayed, For I am thy
3. "When thru the deep wa-ters I call thee to go, The riv-ers of
4. "When thru fi-ery tri-als thy path-way shall lie, My grace, all-suf-
5. "The soul that on Je-sus hath leaned for re-pose, I will not, I

faith in His ex-cel-lent Word! What more can He say than to
God, I will still give thee aid; I'll strength-en thee, help thee, and
woe shall not thee o-ver-flow; For I will be with thee thy
fi-cient, shall be thy sup-ply; The flame shall not hurt thee— I
will not de-sert to his foes; That soul, tho all hell should en-

you He hath said— To you, who for ref-uge to Je-sus have fled?
cause thee to stand, Up-held by my gra-cious, om-nip-o-tent hand.
trou-bles to bless, And sanc-ti-fy to thee thy deep-est dis-tress.
on-ly de-sign Thy dross to con-sume and thy gold to re-fine.
deav-or to shake, I'll nev-er— no, nev-er— no, nev-er for-sake!"

Alternate tunes: ADESTE FIDELES–100, ST. DENIO–34

The LORD God loves us and has established a plan in His Word, the Holy Bible, for people to have their sins forgiven. Through this they will be saved and will be blessed to live with God eternally in Heaven. God the Father established this plan from the foundation of the world and sent His only begotten Son, Jesus Christ, to die on the cross and rise again the third day for the sins of mankind so that through Christ's redemption man might be saved.

John 3:16-17 *For God so loved the world, that he gave his only begotten Son, that whosoever believeth in him should not perish, but have everlasting life. For God sent not his Son into the world to condemn the world; but that the world through him might be saved.*

Colossians 1:14 *In whom we have redemption through his blood, even the forgiveness of sins.*

I Peter 1:18-20 *Forasmuch as ye know that ye were not redeemed with corruptible things, as silver and gold, from your vain conversation received by tradition from your fathers; But with the precious blood of Christ, as of a lamb without blemish and without spot: Who verily was foreordained before the **foundation** of the world, but was manifest in these last times for you, Who by him do believe in God, that raised him up from the dead, and gave him glory; that your faith and hope might be in God.*

We will all stand before God, and only those who have been saved by receiving Jesus Christ into their hearts will enter Heaven.

Hebrews 9:26-27 *For then must he often have suffered since the **foundation** of the world: but now once in the end of the world hath he appeared to put away sin by the sacrifice of himself. And as it is appointed unto men once to die, but after this the judgment:*

The Lord knows those who have been saved and those who belong to Him.

II Timothy 2:19 *Nevertheless the **foundation** of God standeth sure, having this seal, The Lord knoweth them that are his. And, Let every one that nameth the name of Christ depart from iniquity.*

Jesus Christ will separate the saved from the lost. The saved will enter into the kingdom of Heaven, and the lost will suffer in Hell.

Matthew 25:31-34 *When the Son of man shall come in his glory, and all the holy angels with him, then shall he sit upon the throne of his glory: And before him shall be gathered all nations: and he shall separate them one from another, as a shepherd divideth his sheep from the goats: And he shall set the sheep on his right* *hand, but the goats on the left. Then shall the King say unto them on his right hand, Come, ye blessed of my Father, inherit the kingdom prepared for you from the **foundation** of the world:*

Salvation is a free gift. There is nothing we can do ourselves to work our way to Heaven; not by doing good works, attending church or being baptized. Only by trusting Jesus Christ and believing in Him as our personal Savior can we be assured of a home in Heaven.

Ephesians 2:8-9 *For by grace are ye saved through faith; and that not of your-selves: it is the gift of God: Not of works, lest any man should boast.*

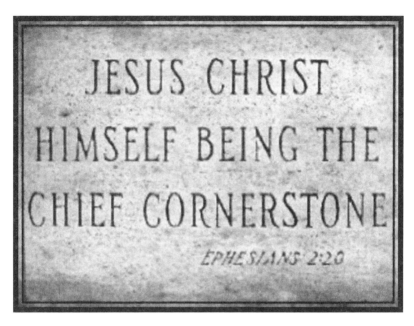

Jesus Christ Himself Is Both the Foundation and the Cornerstone.

I Corinthians 3:9-13 *For we are labourers together with God: ye are God's husbandry, ye are God's building. According to the grace of God which is given unto me, as a wise masterbuilder, I have laid the **foundation**, and another buildeth thereon. But let every man take heed how he buildeth thereupon. For other **foundation** can no man lay than that is laid, which is Jesus Christ. Now if any man build upon this **foundation** gold, silver, precious stones, wood, hay, stubble; Every man's work shall be made manifest: for the day shall declare it, because it shall be revealed by fire; and the fire shall try every man's work of what sort it is.*

Ephesians 2:19-22 *Now therefore ye are no more strangers and foreigners, but fellowcitizens with the saints, and of the household of God; And are built upon the **foundation** of the apostles and prophets, Jesus Christ himself being the chief corner stone; In whom all the building fitly framed together groweth unto an holy temple in the Lord: In whom ye also are builded together for an habitation of God through the Spirit.*

The Solid Rock

EDWARD MOTE, 1797-1874

WILLIAM B. BRADBURY, 1816-1868

1. My hope is built on noth-ing less Than Je-sus' blood and right-eous-ness;
2. When dark-ness veils His love-ly face, I rest on His un-chang-ing grace;
3. His oath, His cov-e-nant, His blood Sup-port me in the whelm-ing flood;
4. When He shall come with trum-pet sound, O may I then in Him be found,

I dare not trust the sweet-est frame, But whol-ly lean on Je-sus' name.
In ev-'ry high and storm-y gale My an-chor holds with-in the veil.
When all a-round my soul gives way, He then is all my hope and stay.
Dressed in His right-eous-ness a-lone, Fault-less to stand be-fore the throne.

REFRAIN

On Christ, the sol-id Rock, I stand— All oth-er ground is

sink-ing sand, All oth-er ground is sink-ing sand.

The wise man comes to Christ and is founded on the Rock.

Luke 6:47-49 *Whosoever cometh to me, and heareth my sayings, and doeth them, I will shew you to whom he is like: He is like a man which built an house, and digged deep, and laid the **foundation** on a rock: and when the flood arose, the stream beat vehemently upon that house, and could not shake it: for it was founded upon a rock. But he that heareth, and doeth not, is like a man that with-out a **foundation** built an house upon the earth; against which the stream did beat vehemently, and immediately it fell; and the ruin of that house was great.*

I Timothy 6:19 *Laying up in store for themselves a good **foundation** against the time to come, that they may lay hold on eternal life.*

Are you saved? Are you sure you will go to Heaven when you die? Have you accepted that free gift of eternal life? God is not willing that any should perish.

II Peter 3:9 *The Lord is not slack concerning his promise, as some men count slackness; but is longsuffering to us-ward, not willing that any should perish, but that all should come to repentance.*

The following verses explain how you can accept Jesus Christ as your personal Savior and receive the free gift of salvation and eternal life in Heaven.

Every person in the world is born with a sin nature so that you cannot escape sinning. You must realize you are a sinner and cannot save yourself.

Romans 3:23 *For all have sinned, and come short of the glory of God.*

Romans 5:12 *Wherefore, as by one man sin entered into the world, and death by sin; and so death passed upon all men, for that all have sinned.*

Because you are a sinner, God cannot accept you into His Holy presence. You are condemned to death, which means eternal separation from God in Hell. The good news is that you do not have to go there, because God has provided a way for you to have eternal life through the redeeming blood of His Son, Jesus Christ.

Romans 6:23 *For the wages of sin is death; but the gift of God is eternal life through Jesus Christ our Lord.*

God loved you so much that He gave His only begotten Son, Jesus Christ, to bear your sin and die in your place.

II Corinthians 5:21 *For he hath made him to be sin for us, who knew no sin; that we might be made the righteousness of God in him.*

The sinless Savior, Jesus Christ, paid the penalty of your sin, by shedding His own blood and dying on the cross for you. He became sin for you.

II Corinthians 5:21 *For he hath made him to be sin for us, who knew no sin; that we might be made the righteousness of God in him.*

Romans 5:8-9 *But God commendeth his love toward us, in that, while we were yet sinners, Christ died for us. Much more then, being now justified by his blood, we shall be saved from wrath through him.*

Jesus Christ is knocking at your heart's door. Won't you let him in?

Revelation 3:20 *Behold, I stand at the door, and knock: if any man hear my voice, and open the door, I will come in to him, and will sup with him, and he with me.*

Our time on earth is short. Don't delay this most important decision. No one has the promise of tomorrow.

James 4:14 *Whereas ye know not what shall be on the morrow. For what is your life? It is even a vapour, that appeareth for a little time, and then vanisheth away.*

Receive Christ into your heart today.

II Corinthians 6:2 *For he saith, I have heard thee in a time accepted, and in the day of salvation have I succoured thee: behold, now is the accepted time; behold, now is the day of salvation.*

Believe on the name of Jesus Christ, confessing with your mouth a prayer of salvation.

Romans 10:9-10 *That if thou shalt confess with thy mouth the Lord Jesus, and shalt believe in thine heart that God hath raised him from the dead, thou shalt be saved. For with the heart man believeth unto righteousness; and with the mouth confession is made unto salvation.*

Call upon the name of the Lord and be saved.

Romans 10:13 *For whosoever shall call upon the name of the Lord shall be saved.*

Psalms 86:5 *For thou, Lord, art good, and ready to forgive; and plenteous in mercy unto all them that call upon thee.*

I John 1:9 *If we confess our sins, he is faithful and just to forgive us our sins, and to cleanse us from all unrighteousness.*

Let God save you this very moment. Pray the following prayer in your heart with all sincerity unto the LORD.

Dear LORD Jesus, I know I am a sinner who cannot stand before a Holy God but deserves to spend an eternity separated from You forever in Hell. I believe, LORD Jesus, You died on the cross, You were buried, and You rose again the third day to pay the penalty for my sin. I am placing my faith and trust in You alone, asking for the gift of eternal life which You purchased for me with Your own blood on the cross. Please come into my heart and be the Master of my life and the Savior of my soul. I am sorry for my sins, and ask You to forgive me, and to take me to Heaven when I die. Thank You, LORD Jesus, for the gift of salvation and everlasting life. In the name of the LORD Jesus Christ I pray. Amen.

Rock of Ages.
"Simply to Thy cross I cling."

—— Toplady

Rock of Ages

TOPLADY

Augustus M. Toplady, 1740-1778   Thomas Hastings, 1784-1872

1. Rock of a - ges, cleft for me, Let me hide my-self in Thee;
2. Could my tears for - ev - er flow, Could my zeal no lan-guor know,
3. While I draw this fleet-ing breath, When my eyes shall close in death,

Let the wa - ter and the blood, From Thy wound-ed side which flowed,
These for sin could not a - tone— Thou must save, and Thou a - lone:
When I rise to worlds un-known And be-hold Thee on Thy throne,

Be of sin the dou-ble cure, Save from wrath and make me pure.
In my hand no price I bring, Sim - ply to Thy cross I cling.
Rock of A - ges, cleft for me, Let me hide my-self in Thee.

243

Chapter Ten

Foundations of Focus

Sundial, Mount Vernon

Clarity of one's thoughts, motives, and actions depends on that one's focus. Someone has stated that if you aim at nothing, you will certainly hit it. America was founded on families whose focus in life was clarified by looking to God's Word, the Holy Bible. George Washington's parents knew the importance of the proper focus for life and so gave him devotional books in his youth. One of these books, *Contemplations Moral and Divine* 1685 by Sir Matthew Hale, was in George Washington's library at his death. It bears the appearance of frequent use with marks of reference, and was known to be one of the books his mother would read to her children and grandchildren; her signature being within its pages. Her focus was not just measured by days or years, but it was measured by eternity. Travel back in time to the sitting room of Mrs. Mary Ball Washington in the 1700s and sense the family's anticipation as she takes a seat in her favorite chair with book in hand. She opens her much worn volume to a marked page, clears her throat, and begins to read.

Portrait of Mary Ball Washington Painted from Life, by Robert Edge Pine in 1786

Contemplations

Moral

And

Divine:

In two Parts.
By Sir Matthew Hale, *Knight*;
late Chief Justice of the Kings-Bench.
LONDON,
1685
(Old English spelling and grammar as published)

Of the Consideration of our
LATTER END,
And the Benefits of it.

pp. 1-11

Deut. XXXII. 29.

O that they were wise, that they understood this,
that they would consider their Latter End!

...the words contain an evident truth, with relation to every particular Person, and to that latter End that is common to all Mankind; namely, their *latter end by death*, and separation of the Soul and Body; the due consideration whereof is a great part of Wisdom, and a great means to attain and improve it; and very many of the sins and follies of Mankind, as they do in a great measure proceed from the want of an attentive and serious consideration of it, so would they be in a great measure cured by it.

It is the *most certain, known, experience truth* in the World, *that all men must die;* that the time of that death is uncertain; that yet most certainly it will come, and that within the compass of no long time: Though the time of our Life might be protracted to its longest period, yet it is ten thousand to one that it will not exceed fourscore years; where one man attains to that age, ten thousand die before it:

...

1. That Men are not willing to entertain this unwelcome thought of their own latter End; the thought whereof is so unwelcome and troublesome a Guest, that it seems to blast and disparage all those present enjoyments of Sense, that this Life affords: Whereby it comes to pass; that as Death it self is unwelcome when it draws near; so the thoughts and pre-apprehensions of it become as unwelcome as the thing it self...

...

3. A great difficulty that ordinarily attends our humane condition, to think otherwise concerning our condition than what at present we feel and find. We are now in health, and we can hardly bring our selves to think that a time must and will come, wherein we shall be sick: We are now in life, and therefore we can hardly cast our thoughts into such a mould, to think we shall die; and hence it is true, as the common Proverb is, *That there is no Man so old, but he thinks he shall live a year longer.*

...

1. It is a great monition and *warning* of us *to avoid Sin*, and a great means to prevent it. When I shall consider that certainly I must die, and I know not how soon, why should I commit those things, that if

they hasten not my Latter End, yet they will make it more uneasy and troublesome by the reflection upon what I have done amiss? I may die to morrow; why should I commit that evil that will then be gall and bitterness unto me? would I do it if I were to die to morrow? why should I then do it to day? perchance it may be the last Act of my Life, and however let me not conclude so ill; for, for ought I know, it may be my concluding Act in this Scene of my Life...

...

A wise and due consideration of our Latter Ends is neither to render us a sad, melancholy, disconsolate People; nor to render us unfit for the Businesses and Offices of our Life; but to render us more watchful, vigilant, industrious, soberly chearful and thankful to that God, that hath been pleased thus to make our lives serviceable to Him, comfortable to us, profitable to others, and after all this to take away the bitterness and sting of Death through Jesus Christ our Lord.

Of the Knowledge of
CHRIST CRUCIFIED.

pp. 36-98

I. Cor. II. 2.

For I determined not to know any thing among you, save Jesus Christ, and him Crucified.

As the *Understanding* is the highest Faculty of the Reasonable Creature, because upon it depends the Regularity of the Motions or Actings of the Will and Affections: So Knowledge is the properest and noblest act or habit of that Faculty, and without which it is without its proper end and employment, and the whole Man without a due guidance and direction, Hos. 4.6...

And as Knowledge is the proper business of that great Faculty, so *the Value of* that *Knowledg*, or employment of the Understanding, is *diversified* according to the Subject about which it is exercised: For though all Knowledg of the most differing Subjects, agree in this *one common Excellence, viz.* the right representation of the thing as it is, unto the Understanding; or the conformity of the Image created in the Understanding, unto the thing objectly united to it, which is *Truth* in the

Understanding: Yet it must needs be, that *according to the various values and degrees of the things* to be known, there ariseth a diversity of the value or worth of that knowledg; that which is of a thing more noble, useful, precious, must needs be a more noble, useful, precious Knowledg, and accordingly, more to be desired.

...the Apostle, among the many things that are to be known, fixeth in the same One thing necessary to be known, Christ Jesus and him Crucified.

Paul Writing His Epistles

Painting attributed to Valentin de Boulogne, 17th century.

There are three steps:

I. Not to know anything. Not as if all *other knowledge* were condemned: *Moses's* Learning was not charged upon him as a sin; *Paul's* secular Learning was not condemned, but useful to him; to be knowing in our calling, in the qualities and dispositions of persons, in the Laws under which we live, in the modest and sober enquiries of nature and Arts, are not only not condemned, but commended, and useful, and such as tend to the setting forth the Glory of the God of Wisdom... But ...we are to esteem that knowledg of other things, otherwise excellent, useful, admirable, yet to be but folly and vile in comparison of the knowledg of Christ. And *this requires*:

A true and right Estimate of the *Value of the knowledg of Christ Jesus above other knowledg...*

1. *In the certainty of it.* Most *other knowledges* are either such as we take in *by our Sense and Experience;* and therein, though it is true, that the gross part of our knowledg, that is nearest to our sense, hath somewhat of certainty in it, yet when we come to sublimate, and collect, and infer that knowledg into universal or general conclusions, or to make deductions, ratiocinations, and determinations from them; then we fail, and hence grew the difference between many Philosophers...But in the knowledg of Christ, we have greater certainty than can be found in any of all these other Knowledges.

1. A constant tradition and reception by millions, before he came, that the *Messias* was to come; and since he came, that in truth he is come. 2. The Apostles, Evangelists, and Disciples, that were purposely chosen to be Witnesses of Christ's Miracles, Doctrine, Suffering, and Resurrection. 3. The Miracles he did, that are witnessed to us, by a greater consent of testimony, than any one part of any History of that Antiquity. 4. The Purity, Sanctity, and Justness of his Doctrine, which was never attained unto in the teaching of the Philosophers, nor ever any could, in the least measure, impeach or blame. 5. The prophecies, stiled most justly by the Apostle a more certain evidence, than the very Vision of his Transfiguration, and a Voice from heaven, 2 Pet. 1. 18. And so in truth is a more undeniable Argument than any is; for it is not capable of any fraud or imposture

...

2. As in the certainty, so *in the Plainness and Easiness of the Truth.* The most excellent Subjects of other knowledg have long windings, before a Man can come at them; and are of that difficulty and abstruseness that as every brain is not fit to undertake the acquiring of it, so much pains, labour, industry, advertency, afliduity is required in the best of Judgments, to attain but a competent incasure of it: Witness the studies of Arithmetick, Geometry, natural Philosophy, Metaphysicks, &c. wherein great labour hath been taken to our hands, to make the passage more easie, and yet still are full of difficulty. But in this knowledg it is otherwise: as it is a knowledg fitted for an universal use, the bringing of Mankind to God, so it is fitted with an universal Fitness and convenience for that use, easie, plain, and familiar. *The poor receive the Gospel*, Matth. 11.5. And indeed the plainness of the Doctrine was that which made the wise World stumble at it, and thence it was, that it was hid from the wise and prudent...But thus it pleased God to

chuse a Doctrine of an easie acquisition; 1. That no flesh should glory in his sight, I Cor. 1. 29. 2. That the way to Salvation, being a common thing propounded to all Mankind, might be difficult to none. *Believe, and thy sins be forgiven. Believe, and thou shalt be saved. Believe, and thou shalt be raised up to Glory*, John 6. 40. *This is the Will of him that sent me, that every one that seeth the Son and believeth on him; may have eternal life, and I will raise him up at the last day.*

3. ...as in the Certainty and Plainness, so *in the Sublimity and Loftiness of the Subject*...The pure Will of God; the Son of God and his miraculous Incarnation, Death, Resurrection and Ascension; The great Covenant between the Eternal God and fallen Man made, sealed and confirmed in Christ, his great transaction with the Father in their Eternal Counsel; and since his Ascension, in his continual Intercession for Man; The means of the discharge and satisfaction of the breach of the Law of God; The state of the Soul after death in blessedness or misery: These and many of these are the subject of that knowledg that is revealed in the knowledg of Christ, such as their very matter speaks them to be of a most high nature...such as the very Angels of Heaven desire to look down into, I Pet. 1.12. And behold with admiration that manifold wisdom of God, which is revealed unto us, poor worms, in Christ Jesus.

4. As the matters are wonderful high, and sublime, so they are *of most singular Use to be known*...this knowledg of Christ is of singular use, and makes a Man a better Philosopher than the best of Morals in reference thereunto: So it guides me in the management of all Relation: 1. To God; it presents him unto me in that representation that is right, full of Majesty, yet full of Love, which teacheth me Reverence, and yet Access with Boldness, Love and Obedience. 2. To Man; Justice, giving every man his due, for so the Knowledg of Christ teacheth me; Do as ye would be done by; Mercy, to forgive; Compassion, to pity; Liberality, to relieve; Sobriety, in the use of creatures, and yet comfort in the enjoying of them; a right use of the World, and yet a contempt of it; in comparison of my hope. It makes death not terrible, because a most sure passage to Life: Here I find a way to get all my sins pardoned, whereas without this, all the world cannot contrive a Satisfaction for one; I find a way to obtain such a Righteousness as is valuable with God, and perfect before him, even the righteousness of God in Christ. And here I find,

the means, and only means, to avoid the wrath to come, the terrour of the judgment of the great day; everlasting life unto all Eternity, with the Blessed God, and our Lord Jesus Christ, and all the Blessed Angels, and the Spirits of Just men made perfect. Thus this knowledg is useful for this life, and that which is to come, and that in the highest degree; which all other knowledge comes short of, and attains not to any one of the least of these ends.

...

II. Thus concerning the first Consideration: *I determined not to know any thing, viz.* nothing in comparison of this knowledg of Christ, nothing rather than not that; *save Christ Jesus.* and truly well might the Apostle make all other knowledg give place to this; first, for the *Excellency* of it, whereof before: secondly, for the *Amplitude* and *Compass* of it; for though it be so excellent, that a small dram of it is sufficient to heal and save a Soul, if it be a right knowledg as is before observed, yet it is so large, that when the best knowledg hath gone as far as it can, yet there is still *aliquid ultra:* One consideration of it, even the Love of God hath a breadth, and length, and depth, and height, passing knowledg, Eph. 3. 18, 19. and yet there be other depths and heights in it than this; so that well might the Apostle conclude as he doth, I Tim. 3.16. *Without controversie great is the mystery of Godliness, God manifested in the flesh.* Therefore for the present we shall consider.

1. The *wonderful* Wisdom *of God in contriving and ordering the redemption of Mankind by Jesus Christ;* and it is manifested in these particulars among others:

1. Though he made Man the eminentest of all his visible Creatures, for a most eminent manifestation of his Power and Glory, and to be partaker of everlasting blessedness, and yet in his Eternal Counsel resolved to leave him in the hands of his own liberty, and did most certainly foresee that he would fall; yet he did substitute and provide, even from the same Eternity, a means whereby he might be restored to the Honour and Glory of his Creature, and his Creature to Blessedness and the Vision of his Creation. 2. That he so ordered the means of Man's Redemption, that a greater Glory came even by that Redemption, than if a man had never faln, and a greater benefit to mankind: For the latter it is apparent, that if there had been no Mediator sent, the least sin that any of the Sons of men had committed, had been inexorably fatal to them, without any means of pardon: And as *Adam;* though in his full liberty and power, was misled by temptation, so might have he

been, or any of his posterity though he had stood that shock; which now is admirably provided against, by the satisfaction of Christ Jesus: And as thus it is better with the Children of men, so the Glory of God is wonderfully advanced by it; for, if man had stood in his innocence, God had had only the Glory of his Justice in Rewarding him; or, if he had faln, the Glory of his Justice in Punishing him: but there had been no room for that glorious Attribute of his Mercy in forgiving, without violation to his Purity, Truth and Justice; that glorious Attribute by which he so often proclaimeth himself, Exod. 34.6. *The Lord, the Lord God, Merciful, Gracious, Long-suffering, abundant in Goodness and Truth, keeping Mercy for thousands, forgiving iniquity, transgression and sin, and yet that will by no means clear the guilty.* 3. That he so wonderfully ordered the Redemption of Man, that all his Attributes were preserved inviolable: His Truth, *the day thou eatest thou shalt dye;* His Justice; yet his Mercy; His Love to his Creatures, yet His hatred to Sin: His Son shall dye to satisfie His Truth and Justice, yet the sinner shall live, to satisfie his Mercy: the sin shall be punished, to justifie His Purity, yet his creature shall be saved, to manifest his Love and Goodness. And thus His Wisdom over-ruled Sin, the worst of evils, to the improvement of His Glory, and the Good of His creature. 4. His Wisdom is manifested in this, that by the Redemption of Man, all those ways of His administration before the coming of Christ, do now appear to be excellently ordered to the Redemption of Man, and the making of it the more effectual: The giving of a severe and yet most just Law, which was impossible for us to fulfil, shews us the wretchedness of our condition; our inability to fulfil, what was just in God to require, shews us the necessity of a Saviour, drives us to him, and makes this City of Refuge grateful and acceptable, and makes us set a value upon that Mercy, which so opportunely and mercifully provided a Sacrifice for us in the Blood of Christ: and a Righteousness for us in the Merits of Christ; and a Mediator for us in the Intercession of Christ: And by this means also all those Sacrifices, and Ceremonies, and Observations enjoyned in the Levitical Law, which carried not in themselves a clear reason of their Institution, are now by the sending of Christ rendred significant. 5. The Wisdom of God is magnified and advanced in this, in fulfilling the Prophecies of the sending the *Messias* to satisfie for the sins of Mankind, against all the oppositions and casualties, and contingencies, that without an over-ruling wisdom and guidance might have disappointed it: And this done, in that Perfection, that not one Circumstance of Time, Place, Person,

Concomitants should or did fail in it: and so bearing witness to the infinite *Truth, Power,* and *Wisdom* of God in bringing about his Counsels in their perfection, touching this great business of the Redemption of Man, which was the very end why he was created and placed upon the earth; and managing the villany of men, and the craft and malice of Satan, to bring about that greatest blessing that was or could be provided for Mankind, besides, and above, and against the intention of the Instrument.

Acts 2.23. *Him being delivered by the determinate councel and foreknowledg of God, ye have taken, and by wicked hands have crucified and slain.* 6. The unsearchable Wisdom of God is manifested in that he provided such a Mediator that was fit for so great a work; had all the world consulted that God must suffer, it had been impossible; and had all the world contributed that any man, or all the men in the world should have been a satisfactory Sacrifice for any one Sin, it had been deficient. Here is then the wonderful Counsel of the most high God: the Sacrifice that is appointed shall be so ordered, that God and Man shall be conjoyned in one Person; that so as Man, he might become a Sacrifice for Sin; and as God, that might give a value to the Sacrifice. And this is the great Mystery of Godliness, God manifested in the flesh.

2. *The wonderful Love of God to Mankind.*

1. In thinking upon poor sinful creatures, to contrive a way for a pardon for us, and rescuing us from that Curse which we had justly deserved. 2. Thinking of us for our good, when we sought it not, thought not of it. 3. When we were enemies against God, and against his very Being. 4. Thinking of us not only for a Pardon, but to provide for us a state of Glory, and Blessednes-s. 5. When that was not to be obtained, saving his Truth and Justice, without a miraculous Mediator, consisting of the Divine and Humane Nature united in one Person, in the person of our Lord Jesus Christ; here was Love and Goodness of the greatest magnitude that ever was, or ever shall be heard of, and sufficient to conquer our hearts into admiration and astonishment. But yet it rests not here...*God so loved the World, that he gave his only begotten Son, that whosoever believeth in him, should not perish, but have everlasting life:* John 3.16. So the only begotten Son of God was not behind in this wonderful Love. No sooner (as we may with reverence say) was the Councel of the Father propounded for the sending of his Son, but presently the Son saith, *Lo, I come,* Psal. 40. 7. Heb. 10.7. And now we will consider upon *what terms* he must come, or else the Redemption of Mankind must dye for ever:

Adoration of the Shepherds by *Gerard van Honthorst* (1622)

1. He must come and empty himself of his Glory, of his personal Majesty, and take our Nature, yet without sin; he must go through the natural infirmities of infancy and childhood. 2. And not only must he undergo this abasement, but he must undergo the condition of a mean, a low birth, born of a poor Virgin, in a Stable, laid in a Manger, under the reputation of a Carpenter's Son. 3. And not only thus, but as soon as he is born, must use the care of his Mother to shift for his life away to *Egypt*, to prevent the jealousie and fury of *Herod*. 4. And when grown up to youth, he must undergo the form of a Servant, become a poor Carpenter to work for his living, without any patrimony, or so much as a House to cover him. 5. He comes abroad into the World to exercise the Ministry, and the Prologue of his own Tragedy; still poor, despised of his own Countreymen, and of those that were of reputation for Learning and Piety, scandalized under the name of an Impostor, a Winebibber, a friend to Publicans and Sinners, a worker by the Devil, mad and possessed with a Devil: These and the like were his entertainments in the World; and, which is more, often put to shift for his life; and in sum, what the Prophet predicted concerning him fulfilled to the uttermost: Isa. 53.3. *Despised and rejected of men, a man of sorrows and acquainted with grief*; and all this to befal the Eternal Son of God under the vail of our

flesh: And all this voluntarily undertaken, and cheerfully undergone, even for the sake of his Enemies and those very people from whom he received these indignities.

III. But all these were but small velitations, and conflicts preparatory to the main Battel. We therefore come *to the third Consideration:* Christ Jesus and him *Crucified;* there is the account of the Text: As Christ Jesus is the most worthy Subject of all knowledg, so Christ Jesus under this Consideration, as Crucified, is that which is the fullest of wonder, admiration, love: And therefore let us now take a survey of *Christ Jesus Crucified;* as that is the highest manifestation of his love, so it is the eye, the life of the Text; Christ above all other knowledg, and Christ Crucified above all other knowledg of Christ.

And now a Man upon the first view would think this kind of knowledg, so much here valued, were a strange kind of knowledg, and the prelation of this knowledg a strange mistake in the Apostle. 1. *Crucified*: Death is the corruption of nature: And such a kind of Death by Crucifixion, the worst, the vilest of Deaths, carrying in it the punishment of the lowest: condition of men, and for the worst of offences; and yet, that Death and such a Death should be the ambition of an Apostle's knowledg, is wonderful. 2. *Christ Crucified;* carries in it a seeming excess of incongruity; that he, that was the Eternal Son of God, should take upon him our Nature, and in that Nature anointed and consecrated by the Father, full of Innocence, Purity, Goodness, should die, and that by such a death, and so unjustly; Could this be a subject, or matter of knowledg so desireable, as to be preferred before all other knowledg? which should rather seem to be a matter of so much horrour, so much indignation, that a man might think it rather fit to be forgotten, than to be affected to be known. 3. *Jesus Crucified.* A Saviour and yet to be Crucified; it seems to blast the expectation of Salvation; when the Captain of it must die, be slain, be crucified; it carries in it a kind of victory of Death and Hell over our Salvation, when the instrument thereof must suffer Death, and such a Death. When the birth of Christ was proclaimed, indeed it was matter of joy, and worth the proclamation of Angels: Luke 2.12. *To you is born this day a Saviour, which is Christ the Lord,* and can the death of that Saviour be a thing desireable to be known? the Birth of Christ seemed to be the rising Sun, that scattered light, hope and comfort to all nations: but can the setling of this Sun in so dark a cloud as the Cross, be the choicest piece of knowledg of him?

which seems as it were to strangle and stifle our hopes; and puts us as it were upon the expostulation of the dismay'd Disciples, Luke 24. 21. *But we trusted it had been he which should have redeemed Israel.*

But for all this, this knowledg of Christ Jesus Crucified will appear to be the most excellent, comfortable, useful knowledg in the world, if we shall consider *these Particulars*: **1. Who it was that suffered. 2. What he suffered. 3. From whom 4. How he suffered. 5. For whom he suffered. 6. Why, and upon what motive**...All these *Considerations* are wrapt up in this one subject; Christ Jesus and him crucified.

I. *Who it was that thus suffered.* It was Christ Jesus the Eternal Son of God, cloathed in our flesh; God and Man united in one Person; his Manhood giving him a Capacity of suffering, and his Godhead giving a Value to that suffering; and each Nature united in one Person to make a compleat Redeemer; the Heir of all things,; Heb. 1.2. The Prince of Life; Acts. 3.15. the Light that lightneth every man that cometh into the world; John 1.9. As touching his Divine Nature, God over all blessed for ever; Rom. 9.5. And as touching his Humane Nature, full of Grace and Truth; John 1.14. And in both the beloved Son of the Eternal God, in whom he proclaimed himself well pleased, Matth. 3.17. But could no other person be found, that might suffer for the sins of Man, but the Son of God? Or if the business of our Salvation must be transacted by him alone, could it not be without suffering, and such suffering as this? No. As there was no other Name given under Heaven, by which we might be saved, nor was there any found besides, in the compass of the whole World, that could expiate for one sin of Man; but it must be the Arm of the Almighty, that must bring Salvation: Isa. 63.5. So if the blessed Son of God will undertake the business, and become Captain of our Salvation, he must be made perfect by suffering, Heb. 2.10. And if he will stand in the stead of Man, he must bear the wrath of his Father: If he will become sin for Man, though he knew no sin, he must become a curse for Man. And doubtless this great Mystery of the Person that suffered, cannot choose but be a very high and excellent subject of Knowledg; so full of wonder and astonishment, that the Angels gaze into it: And as it is a strange and wonderful thing in it self, so doubtless it was ordained to high and wonderful ends, bearing a suitableness unto the greatness of the Instrument. This therefore is the first Consideration that advanceth the excellency of this knowledg; the Person that was crucified.

II. *What he suffered.* Christ Jesus and him crucified; though all the course of his life was a continual suffering, and the preamble or walk unto his death, which was the end of his life; yet this was the completing of all the rest, and the Tide and Waves of his sufferings did still rise higher and higher, till it arrived in this: and the several steps and ascents unto the Cross though they began from his Birth, yet those that were more immediate, began with the preparation to the Passover. The Council held by the chief Priests and Scribes, for the crucifying of our Saviour, was sat upon two days before the Passover, Matth. 26.2. Mark 14.1. And this was the first step to Mount Calvary: And doubtless it was no small addition to our Saviour's Passion, that it was hatched in the Councel of the chief Priests and Scribes, the then external visibly Church, the Husbandmen of the Vineyard: Matth. 21.33. But this is not all; as the visible Church of the Jews is the Conclave where this Council is formed; So Judas a Member of the visible Church of Christ, one of the Twelve, is the Instrument to effect it; Matth. 26.14. He contracts with them for Thirty pieces of Silver, to betray his Master unto them: And surely this could not choose but be a great grief to our Saviour, that one of his select Apostles should turn Apostate, and thereby brought a blemish upon the rest.

Upon the day of Eating the Passover, called the first day of the Feast of unleavened Bread, our Saviour and his Disciples keep the Passover together in *Jerusalem*; and there the two Memorials of our Saviours Passion meet: that of the Passover instituted by God, and the *Israelites* going out of *Egypt*; and the Bread and Wine after Supper instituted by our Saviour, to succeed in the place of the former: and each did questionless make a deep impression upon our Saviour, in which he anticipated his Passion, and lively represented to him that breaking and pouring out his Blood and Soul, which he was suddenly to suffer: And doubtless here began a great measure of our Saviour's Passion, in the apprehension which he had of that eminent Storm, that he must speedily undergo. From the Supper they go together to the Mount of *Olives*, and there he acquaints his Disciples of a speedy and sorrowful parting they must have; the Shepherd is to be smitten that night, and the Sheep to be scattered: and as he foresaw *Judas's* treachery, so he foresees *Peter's* infirmity; the Storm should be so violent, that *Peter* himself, the resolutest Apostle, shall deny his Master that night, and deny him thrice:

Statue of Peter Denying Christ
(© T.M. Creed)

And surely the foresight of the distraction that should befal his poor Disciples, could not choose but add much to their tender Master's affliction, Matth. 26.31. *all ye shall be offended because of me this night.*

And now let us follow our Blessed Lord from the Mount of *Olives* into the Garden, called by the Apostles *Gethsemane*, with the affection of love and wonder, in some measure becoming such an entertainment of our thoughts. The time that he chose for this retirement was the dead time of the night; a season that might the more contribute to the strength of that sadness, which the pre-apprehension of his imminent Passion, must needs occasion. The place that he chose, a solitary retired Garden, where nothing might, nor could interrupt, or divert the intensiveness of his sorrow and fear: And to make both the time and place the more opportune for his Agony, he leaves the rest of his Disciples, and takes with him only *Peter* and the two Sons of *Zebedee*, Matth. 26.37. And to these he imparts the beginning of his sorrow, that they might be witnesses of it, Matth. 26:37. *My Soul is exceeding sorrowful, even unto death;* but yet commands their distance, verse 38. *Tarry ye here and watch with me, and he went a little further. Watch with me:* The confusion of his Soul was so great, that the only Son of God distrusts his own (humane) ability to bear it; and yet his submission to this terrible conflict (was) so willing, that he leaves them that he had appointed to watch with him. *He went a little farther.* The three disciples had doubtless a sympathy with their Master's sorrow, and yet the Will of God so orders it, that their excess of love and grief must not keep their Eyes waking, notwithstanding it was the last request of their sorrowful Master. *The Disciples slept,* Matth. 26.40. And thus every circumstance of Time, Place, and Persons contribute to a sad and solitary opportunity for this most terrible and black conflict. And now in this Garden the mighty God puts his Son to grief, lades him with our sorrows, Isa. 53.4, withdraws and hides from him the light of his favour and countenance; interposeth a thick and black cloud between the Divinity and the Humane Nature; darts into his Soul the sad and sharp manifestations of his wrath; overwhelms his Soul with one wave after another; sends into him the most exquisite pre-apprehensions of those sad and severe sufferings he was the next day to undergo; begins to make his Soul an Offering for Sin, and heightens his sorrow, confusion, and astonishment unto the uttermost. In sum, the mighty God, the God of the spirits of all flesh, who knows the way into the Soul, and how to fill it with the most sad and black astonishment and sorrow, was pleased at this time to estrange and eclipse the manifestation of his light and love to his only Son, as far as was possibly consistent with his secret and eternal love unto him; to throw into him as sad and amazing apprehensions of his wrath, as was possible to be consistent with the Humane Nature to bear; to fortifie and strengthen his sense of it, and sorrow for, and under it, unto the uttermost, that so his grief and sorrow and confusion of Soul might be brim-ful, and as much as the exactest constitution of a Humane Nature could possibly bear. And thus now at this time the Arm of the mighty God was bruising the Soul of his only Son: Isa. 53.6. And certainly the extremity of this agony within, must needs be very great, if we consider the strange effects it had without: 1.

That pathetical description thereof that our Saviour himself makes of it; *My Soul is exceeding sorrowful, even unto death,* Matth. 26.37. so sorrowful, exceeding sorrowful, sorrowful unto death, and the expressions of the Evangelists, Matth. 26.37. *He began to be sorrowful, and very heavy.* Mark 14.33. *He began to be sore amazed, and to be very heavy.* It was such a sorrow as brought with it an amazement, an astonishment. 2. Again, that strange request to his three Disciple, *Tarry ye and watch with me;* as if he feared the sorrow would overwhelm him. 2. Again, his Prayer, and the manner of it, evidence a most wonderful perturbation within, Matth. 26.39. *He fell on his face and prayed;* and what was the thing he prayed? *Father if it be possible, let this Cup pass from me;* or as Mark 14.36. *Abba Father, all things are possible unto thee, take away this Cup from me,* &c. Although that this was the very end for which he came into the world: The Cup which in former times he reached after, and was straitned till it were fulfilled; yet such a representation there is thereof to his Soul, that although in the Will of his obedience, he submits; *Not my Will but thine be done:* Yet his nature shrinks and starts at it; and he engageth Almighty God, as much as, upon as great arguments as was possible, to decline the severity of that wrath which he was now to grapple with: 1. Upon the account of his Omnipotency; *All things are possible to thee:* 2. Upon the account of his Relation; *Abba, Father:* It is not a stranger that importunes thee; it is thy Son; that Son in whom thou didst proclaim thy self well pleased; that Son whom thou hearest always; it is he that begs of thee; and begs of thee a dispensation from that which he most declines, because he most loves thee, the terrible, unsupportable hiding thy face from me. And this was not one single request but thrice repeated, reiterated, and that with more earnestness, Mark 14.39. *And again he went away, and prayed, and spake the same words:* Luke 22.44. And being in an agony he prayed more earnestly. Certainly, that impression upon his Soul, that caused him to deprecate that for which he was born, to deprecate it so often, so earnestly, must needs be a sorrow and apprehension of a very terrible and exceeding extremity. 4. Such was the weight of his sorrow and confusion of Soul, that it (was) exceeding the strength of his (Humane) Nature to bear it, it was ready to dissolve the Union between his Body and Soul; insomuch that to add farther strength unto him, and capacity to undergo the measure of it, an Angel from Heaven is sent, not (meerly) to comfort, but to strengthen him; to add a farther degree of strength to his Humane Nature, to bear the weight of that wrath, which had in good earnest made his Soul sorrowful unto death, had it not been strengthened by the ministration of an Angel, Luke 22.43. and his assistance of the Angel, as it did not allay the sorrow of his Soul, so neither did it intermit his importunity to be delivered from the thing he felt and feared; but did only support and strengthen him to bear a greater burden of it: and as the measure of his strength was increased, so was the burthen which he must undergo, increased, for after this he prayed again more earnestly the third time, Luke 22.43. The supply of his strength was succeeded with an addition of sorrow, and the increase of his sorrow was followed with the greater importunity; *he prayed more earnestly,* Heb. 5.7. *with strong crying and tears,* Luke 22.44. *And being in Agony, he prayed more earnestly, and his Sweat was it were great drops of Blood falling down to the ground.* This was his third Address to his Father, Matth. 26.44.

And here was the highest pitch of our Saviour's passion in the Garden. His soul was in agony, in the greatest concussion, confusion, and extremity of sorrow, fear, anguish, and astonishment, that was possible to be inflicted by the mighty hand of God on the Soul of Christ, that could be consistent with the purity of the nature of our Saviour, and the inseparable union that it had with the Divine Nature: Insomuch, that the confusion and distraction of his Soul under it, and the strugling and grapling of his Soul with it, did make such an impression upon his Body, that the like was never before or since. The season of the year was cold, for so it appears, John 18.18. The Servants and Officers had made a fire of coals, for it was cold: and the season of the time was cold; it was, as near as we may guess, about midnight, when the Sun was at his greatest distance, and obstructed in his influence by the interposition of the Earth: for it appears they came with Lanthorns and Torches when they apprehended him, John 18.3. and he was brought to the High Priest's hall, a little before Cock-crowing, after some time had been spent in his Examination, Matth. 26.69. And yet for all this, such is the Agony and perturbation of our Saviour's Soul, that in this cold season it puts his body in a sweat, a sweat of blood, great drops of blood, drops of blood falling down to the ground; and certainly it was not light conflict within, that caused such a strange and un-heard of symptom without. Certainly the storm in the Soul of Christ must needs be very terrible, that his blood, the seat of his vital spirits, could no longer abide the sense of it, but started out in a sweat of blood, and such a sweat, that was more than consistent with the ordinary constitution of Humane Nature. And during this time, even from the eating of the Passover until this third address to his Father was over, the suffering of our Saviour lay principally, if not only, in his Soul. Almighty God was wounding of his spirit, and making his Soul an offering for sin: And though the distinct, and clear *manner of this bruising of our Saviour's Soul* cannot be apprehended by us; yet surely thus much we may conclude concerning it: 1. *He was made sin for us,* that knew no sin, 2 Cor. 5.21. He stood under the imputation of all our sins; and though he were personally innocent, yet judicially and by way of interpretation, he was the greatest offender that ever was; *for the Lord laid upon him the iniquity of us all,* Isa. 53.6. 2. and consequently he was under the imputation of all the guilt of all those sins, and stands, in relation unto God, the righteous Judg, under the very same obligation to whatsoever punishment the very persons of the offenders were, unto the uttermost of that consistency that it had with the unseparable union unto the Father: And this obligation unto the punishment could not choose but work the same effects in our Saviour, as it must do in the inner (desperation and sin excepted;) to wit, a sad apprehension of the wrath of God against him. The purity and justice of God, which hath nothing that it hates but sin, must pursue sin, wherever it find it: and as when it finds sin personally in a man, the wrath of God will abide there so long as sin abides there; so when it finds the same sin assumed by our Lord, and bound as it were to him, as wood was to *Isaac,* when he was laid upon the Altar, the wrath of God could not choose but be apprehended as incumbent upon him, till that sin that by imputation lay upon him were discharged. For as our Lord was pleased to be our Representative in bearing our sins, and to stand in our stead, so all these affections and emotions of his Soul did bear the same conformity, as if enacted by us: As he put on the person of the sinner, so he puts on the same sorrow, the same shame, the same fear, the same trembling, under the apprehension of the wrath of his Father, that we must have done: and so as an imputed sin drew with it the obligation unto punishment, so it did, by necessary consequence, raise all those confusions and storms in the Soul of Christ, as it would have done in the person of the sinner, sin only excepted. 3. In this Garden, as he stands under the sin, and guilt of our nature, so he stands under the curse of our nature, to wit, a necessity of death, and of undergoing the wrath of God for that sin whose Punishment he hath undertaken for us: the former, the dissolution of his Body and Soul by a most accursed death; and the latter the *suffering of his Soul*; and this *latter* he is now under. God is pleased to inflict upon him all the manifestations of his wrath, and to fling into his Soul the sharpest and feverest representation of his displeasure that might possibly befal him under that bare imputed guilt considering the dignity of his Person. And surely this was more terrible to our Savior than all his corporal sufferings were: under all those not one word, no perturbation at all, *but as a sheep before his shearers is dumb, so he opened not his mouth:* But the sense of the displeasure of his Father, and the impressions that he makes upon his Soul, those he cannot bear without sorrow, even unto death, without most importune addresses to be delivered from them, and most strange concussion and agony upon his Soul and Body, under the sense of them. And *the actual manifestation of the wrath of God upon his Son* consisted in these two things principally.

Garden of Gethsemane
(© T.M. Creed)

1. Filling the Soul with strange and violent fears and terrors; insomuch that he was in an amazement and consternation of the spirit; the Passion Psalm renders it Psalm 22.14. *My heart is like wax, it is melted in the midst of my Bowels:* The God of the Spirits of all...that knows how to grind and bruise the spirit, did bruise and melt his Soul within him with terrors, fears, and sad pre-apprehensions of worse to follow.

2. A sensible withdrawing, by hasty and swift degrees, the light of the presence and favour of God: He is sorrowful and troubled, and he goes to his Father to desire it may pass from him, but no answer; he goes again, but yet no answer; and yet under the pressure and extremity; he goes again the third time with more earnestness, agony, a sweat of blood; yet no, it cannot be; and this was a terrible condition, that the light of the countenance of the Father is removed from his Son, his only Son, in whom he was well pleased, his Son who he had heard always: And when he comes to the Father under the greatest obligation that can be, with the greatest revenge, with the greatest importunity; once, and again, and a third time; and that, filled within with fears, and covered without with Blood, and yet no answer; but all light, and access with favour intercepted, with nothing but blackness and silence. Certainly this was a terrible Cup, yet thus it was with our Saviour Christ; the light of the favour of God, like the Sun in an Eclipse...began to be covered one degree after another; and in the third address to the Father in the Garden, it was even quite gone: But at that great hour, when our Saviour cried, *My God, my God why hast thou forsaken me?* then both Lights, that greater Light of the favour of God to his only Son, together with the Light of the Sun, seemed to be under a total Eclipse; and this was that which bruised the Soul of our Saviour; and made it an Offering for Sin; and this was that which wrung drops of Blood from our Saviour's Body, before the Thorns, or Whips, or the Nails, or the Spear had torn his veins.

And now after this third application for a deliverance from the terrible Cup of the wrath of God, and yet no dispensation obtained, he returns to his miserable Comforters, the three Disciples; and he finds them a third time asleep: These very three Disciples were once the witnesses of a glorious Transfiguration of our Saviour in the Mount, and in an extasie of joy and fear, they fell on their faces, Mat. 17.6. and now they are to be witnesses of a sad Transfiguration of their Lord under an agony and sweat of blood; and now under an extasie of sorrow they are not able to watch with their Lord one hour. Our Savior calls them, but whiles they were scarce awakened, they are rouzed by a louder alarm, Matth. 26.47. *Whiles he yet spake, Judas, one of the twelve came, and with him a great multitude, with swords and staves from the High Priests, John 18.3. with Lanthorns and Torches:* And though this was little in comparison of the storm that was in our Saviour's Soul; yet such an appearance, at such a time of the night, and to a person under such a sad condition, could not but be terrible to flesh and blood; especially, if we consider the Circumstances that attend it. 1. An Apostle, one of the twelve, he it is that conducts this black Guard, Matt. 26.48. *Whomsoever I shall kiss, that same is he, hold him fast;* one that had been witness of all his Miracles, heard all his Divine Sermons, acquainted with all his retirements; he, whose feet his Master with love and tenderness had washed, who within a few hours before had supped with him, at that Supper of Solemnity and Love, the Passover; this is he that is in the head of this Crew: certainly this had in it an aggravation of sorrow to our Blessed Saviour, to be betrayed by a Disciple. 2. The manner of it, he betrays him by a kiss; an emblem of homage and love is made use of to be the signal of scorn and contempt, as well as treachery and villany. 3. Again, the carriage of his Disciples, full of rashness, and yet of cowardize; they strike a Servant of the High Priest, and cut off his Ear, Matth. 26.51. which had not the meekness and mercy of our Saviour prevented by a miraculous cure, might have added a blemish to the sweetness and innocence of his suffering. He rebukes the rashness of his Disciples, and cures the wound of his Enemy. Again, of Cowardise, Matth. 26.56. *Then all the Disciples forsook him and fled;* and Peter himself, that but now had professed the resolution of his love to his Master, follows, but a-far off, Mat. 26.58. in the posture and profession of a Stranger and a Spectator. So soon was the Love and Honour of a Master, deserved by so much Love, and Purity, and Miracle, lost in the Souls of the Very Disciples.

After this, he is brought to the High Priests, the solemn Assembly of the then visible Church of the Jews, in the Persons of the greatest Reverence and Esteem among them, the High Priests, Scribes, and Elders; and before them Accused, and Convicted of those Crimes that might render Him Odious to the *Jews, Romans,* and all good men; Blasphemy, and by them pronounced worthy of Death, Matth. 26.66. and after this, exposed to the basest usage of the basest of their retinue; the Servants spit on him, buffet him, expose him to Scorn, saying,

Prophesie unto us thou Christ, who is he that smote thee? Mat. 26:67. Injuries less tolerable than Death to an Ingenuous Nature: and, to add to all the rest, Peter, instead of reproving the Insolence of the Abjects, and bearing a part with his Master in his Injuries, thrice denying his Master, and that with an oath and Cursing: so far was he from owning his Master in his Adversity, that he denied he knew him and this in the very presence of our Saviour, Luke 22.61. *And the Lord turned and looked upon Peter;* certainly that look of our Saviour, as it carried a secret message of a gentle reprehension, so also of much sorrow, and grief in our Lord: As if he should have said, *Ah, Peter,* canst thou see thy Saviour thus used and wilt thou not own me? Or if thou wilt not, yet must thou needs deny me, deny me thrice, deny me with Oaths, and with Execrations? The unkindness of a Disciple, and such a Disciple, that hast been privy to my Glory in my Transfiguration, and to my Agony in the Garden, cuts me deeper than the Scorns and Derisions of these Abjects. But that's not all; this Apostacy of thine, these Denials, these Oaths, these Execrations will lie heavy upon me anon, and add to that unsupportable burden that I am under; the Thorns, and the Whips, and the Nails that I must anon suffer, will be the more envenomed by these sins of thine; and thou castest more Gall into that bitter Cup, that I am drinking, than all the Malice of mine Enemies could do. In sum, though thou goest out, and weepest bitterly, yet these Sins of thine would stick unto thy Soul unto Eternity, if I should not bear them for thee; they cost thee some Tears, but they must cost me my Blood.

The next morning the High-Priests and Elders hold a second consultation, as soon as it was day, Luke 22.66. Their Malice was so solicitous, that they prevent the Morning Sun; and after they had again examined him, and in that Council charged him with Blasphemy, the Council and the whole Multitude lead him bound to *Pilate*; and there they accuse him; and, to make their Accusation the more gracious, charge him with Sedition against the *Romans*; and though he had no other Advocate but Silence and Innocence, for he answered them nothing; yet the Judge acquits him...*I find no fault in him;* and yet, to shift his hands of the Employment, and to gratifie an Adversary, he sends him to *Herod*, and his Accusers follow him thither also, Luke 23.10. The Chief Priests and Scribes vehemently Accuse him: *Herod* when he had satisfied his Curiosity in the sight of Jesus, to add to the Scorn of our Saviour, exposeth him to the Derision of his rude Souldiers, and cloaths him in a Gorgeous Robe, and remands him to Pilate. Thus in Triumph and Scorn he is sent from place to place: first to *Annas*; then *Caiphas*; then consented before the Council of the Priests, then sent into the High Priests Hall; then re convented before the Council; then sent bound to *Pilate*; and from thence to *Herod*; and from him back again to *Pilate*: and in those Translations from place to place, exposed unto, and entertained with new Scorns, and Derisions, and Contempts.

At his return to *Pilate*, he again the second time declares his Innocence; that neither he nor *Herod* found any thing worthy of Death, Luke 23.15. And yet to satisfie the *Jews*, he offers to have him Scourged, whom he pronounceth Innocent; yet to avoid the gross injustice of a Sentence of Death, offers to release him, to observe their Custom; but this could not satisfie: To observe their Custom, and yet to fulfil their Malice, they chose the Reprieve of *Barrabbas* a Murderer, and opportune the Crucifying of the Innocent Jesus; and now the third time *Pilate* pronounceth him Innocent, Luke 23.22. and yet delivers him over to be Crucified. The Executioners did it to the uttermost, and to add... scorn to his scourging, put upon him a Crown of Thorns: and in his Disguise of Blood and Contempt, brings him forth, shews him to his Persecutors, John 19,.5. *Behold the Man;* as if he should have said, 'You Jews, that have accused this man, must know I find no fault in him; yet to satisfie your Importunity, I have delivered him over to the severest and vilest punishment next unto Death, Scourging and Scorn; here he is, see what a Spectacle it is, let this satisfie your envy. But all this will not serve, there is nothing now the vilest of Deaths can satisfie; all cry out, *Crucify him:* and when yet the Judge professeth he finds nothing worthy of Death, they impose a Law of their own; *We have a Law, and by our law he ought to dye because he made himself the Son of God,* John 19.7. But when this rather made the Judge the more cautious, they engage him upon his fidelity to Caesar his Master: *He maketh himself a King, speaketh against Caesar:* But all this was not enough; but at length the importunity of the Priests and People prevailed; and Pilate who had been before warned by the monition of his Wife; and had three several times pronounced him innocent, yet against the Conviction of his own Conscience, to satisfie and content the *Jews*, adds this farther Cruelty and Injustice to what he had before done, gave Sentence that it should be as they required, Luke 23.24. delivered him over to that cursed and servile Death of Crucifixion: and yet his Persecutors Malice and Envy not satisfied; but, after his Judgment, pursue the Execution of it with as great Malice, Scorn, and Cruelty, as they had before used in obtaining it: His Crown of Thorns upon his Head; a Purple Robe upon his Body; the Blood of his Scourging, and Thorns all covering his Visage: a Reed in his Right Hand; and the Base and Insolent Multitude with Spittings, and Stroaks, and Reproaches, abusing him, till his Cross be ready: and then the Purple Robe is taken off, and he conducted to the place of his Execution; and, to add Torment to his shame, our Blessed Lord, wearied with an Agony, and long watching the night before; and from the time of his Apprehending hurried from place to place; and his Blood and Spirits spent with the Scourgings and Thorns, and Blows; and, which is more than all this, a Soul within laden with the weight of Sorrow, and the burden of the Wrath of God, which did drink up and consume his Spirits: yet, in this Condition, he is fain to bear his burdensom Cross towards the place of his Execution, John 19.17. till he was able to carry it no longer, but even fainted under it, and then *Simon* of *Cyrene* is compelled to bear it to the place, Mat. 27.32.

Christ was crucified at Golgotha meaning the place of a skull.
(© T.M. Creed)

When he comes to the place of Execution, he is stript stark naked, and his cloaths afterwards divided by lot among the souldiers, Mat. 27.35. and his naked Body stretched upon the Cross to the uttermost extension of it, Psal. 22.17. *I may tell all my Bones, they look and stare upon me:* and at the uttermost Extension, which the cruel Executioners could make of our Saviour's Body, his Hands and his Feet nailed to that Cross, with great Nails, through those tender parts full of Nerves and Arteries, and most exquisitely sensible of pain. and in this condition the Cross with our Saviour's Body is raised up in view of all; and, that even in this his Execution, that the Shame and Ignominy of the manner of his Death might have a farther accession of Scorn and Reproach, he is placed between two Thieves, that were Crucified with him, with an inscription of Derisin upon his Cross, in all the most universal Languages of all the World, *Hebrew, Greek,* and *Latin*; and the People and Priests standing by with Gestures and Words of Derision, Matth. 27. 39, 40. and, even to a Letter, assuming those very Gestures and Words which were so many hundreds of years predicted in the Passion-Psalm 22.7-8. *He trusted in God, let him deliver him, if he will have him;* and one of those very Thieves, that was even dying as a Malefactor, yet was filled with such a Devilish Spirit, that he upbraids and derides him.

And now our Saviour is under the Torments and Shame of this cursed Execution: but, though these his Sufferings of his Body and outward Man, were very grievous, insomuch that it could not but extremely afflict him; yet it is strange to see how little he was transported under them, in all his Contumelies, Reproaches, and Accusations, scarce a word answered; He answered them nothing to all his Abusings, Strokes, Ridiculous Garments, Crown of Thorns, tearing of his Body with Scourging; yet not a word; but *As a Sheep before the Shearers is dumb, so he opened not his mouth;* Isa. 53.7...yet the weight of that Wrath that lay upon his Soul, now made an offering for Sin, did wring from him those bitter and terrible cries, that one would wonder should proceed from him, that was One with the Father, Mat. 27. 46. *My God, my God, why hast thou forsaken me?* From the sixth hour to the ninth darkness was over all the Land. Matth. 27.45...This cry of our Saviour was about the ninth hour, a little before his death, and having fulfilled one Prophecy in this terrible cry, contained in the very words of Psalm 22. he fulfils another, he saith, *I thirst,* John 19. 28. And presently they gave him Vinegar to drink. And *between this and his death there intervene these passages.* 1. His proclaiming to the World, that the work of our Redemption was finished, John 19.30. *When he received the Vinegar, he said, It is finished...*2. A second cry *with a loud voice*, Mat. 27. 50. The Words are not expressed of his second cry; only both Evangelists, *Matthew* and *Luke*, testifie it was a cry with a loud voice; to evidence to the World that in the very Article of his giving up of the Ghost, the strength of Nature was not wholly spent, for he cryed with a loud voice. 3. The comfortable resignation of his Soul into the hands of his Father, Luke 23.46. *Father, into thy hands I commend my Spirit:* and although, but even now the black Storm was upon his Soul, that made him cry out with that loud and bitter cry, yet the Cloud is over, and with comfort he delivers up his Soul into the hands of that God, whom he thought, but even now, had forsaken him. It is more than probable that that bitter cry was uttered at the very *Zenith* of his pains; and when he had taken the Vinegar, and proclaimed that it is finished; though they were all wrapt up in a very small time, about the end of the ninth hour, yet now there remained no more, but for him to give up his Spirit, which he instantly thereupon did, John 19. 30. *He said, it is finished, he bowed the head, and gave up the Ghost.* Now the *things wonderfully observable in the Death of our Saviour* are many. 1. That it was a voluntary delivering up of his Spirit: this is that which he said, Mat. 10. 18. *No man taketh it from me, but I lay it down: I have power to lay it down, and I have power to take it again: this commandment have I received of my Father.* And truly this voluntary delivering up of his Soul, was well near as great an evidence of his Divinity, as his resuming it again: for that this very delivering up of his Soul, Converted the Centurion, Mark. 15. 39. *When he saw that he so cryed and gave up the Ghost, he said, Truly this man was the Son of God...*

And now we have gone thus far with our Lord unto his Death, we shall follow him to *his Grave. Joseph* of *Arimathea*, having an honourable mention by all four Evangelists...goes to *Pilate* boldly, and begs his Saviours Body; he wraps it in a clean Linnen Cloath, laid in a Tomb provided for himself, and hewed out of the Rock, and rolled a great Stone upon the door of the Sepulchre. And as by his Death with the Malefactors, so by his Burial in this Rich man's Sepulchre, he fulfilled both parts of the Prophecy, Isa. 53. 9. *He made his Grave with the Wicked, and with the rich in his Death*. The High Priests continued their malice, and their jealousie, even against the dead body of our Saviour; and, to secure themselves against the suspicion of his Resurrection the third day, take order for making the Sepulchre sure, till the third day was past, Matth. 27.60. They seal the Stone, and set a Watch. And it is very observable, how the Almighty Council of God made use of the very Malice and Jealousie of these People, for the confirming of his own Truth, Christ's Resurrection, and our Faith; Their Malicious and Curious Industry, to prevent the possibility of a fictitious Resurrection, abundantly and uncontrollably convincing the Reality of our Saviour's Death and true Resurrection. He is laid in the Grave the Evening of the day wherein he suffered; a Stone rolled upon the mouth of the Grave, such as required a considerable strength to remove it, insomuch that the women that came the first day of the Week to embalm the Body, were in a great difficulty how it should be removed; Mark 16. 3. For it was a great Stone; Matth. 27. 60. And this Stone Sealed: And, as if all this were too little, and the Bonds of Death and the Grave were too weak, they add a Watch of Soldiers to secure the Body, Matth. 27:66. And here we leave for a while our Saviour's Body interred in Spices...

And now we come to the Consideration *of the Resurrection* of our Lord; by which he was declared to be the Son of God with power; and by which the fulness and compleatness of our Redemption by him, is abundantly manifested...he chose that day to rise again, which his Father chose to begin the Creation, the first day of the Week; that the same day might bear the inscription of the Creation and of the Restitution of the World: And that as in that day the Lord God brought Light out of Darkness, so this Light, the Light that enlightneth every man that comes into the World, should arise from the Land of Darkness, the Grave...An Angel from Heaven comes down to draw the Curtain of our Saviours grave, and with an Earth-quake rolls away the Stone that covered it; the Keepers, who had watchfully observed the Command of their Commanders, were stricken with Astonishment, and became as dead...Our Lord, who had power to lay down his Life, and power to take it up again, John 10. 17. re-assumes his Body, which, though it had tasted Death, yet had not seen Corruption, and ariseth, and thereby proclaimed the compleating of our Redemption; and therefore not possible he should be longer holden of it, Acts 2. 24. his Victory over Death and the Grave for us, I Cor. 15. When our Lord raised up *Lazarus*, he came forth of the Grave bound hand and foot with Grave-Cloaths, John 11. 44. Though he was for the present rescued from Death by the power of Christ, yet he must still be a Subject to it: He is revived, but yet riseth with the Bonds of Death about him; he must die again: But when our Lord riseth, he shakes off his Grave cloaths; the linnen that wrapped his Body in one place, and the Linnen that bound his Head in another, John 20. 6,7. Our Lord being risen, dieth no more; Death hath no power over him, Rom. 6. 9...

The Garden Tomb of Jesus Christ

(© T.M. Creed)

III. *From whom he suffered* all these things....1. He suffered this from the hands of his own Father; it was he that bruised him, put him to grief, and made his Soul an offering for sin, Isa. 53. 10. It was he that reached him out that bitter Cup to drink, John 18. 11. *The Cup which my Father hath given me, shall I not drink?* It was he, that bound that burden so close upon him, that made him sweat great drops of Blood in the Garden, and though thrice importuned for a dispensatin from it, yet would not grant it: it was he, that when the greatest extremity of pain and sorrow lay upon him, to add thereunto, withdrew the sense of his presence from him, which wrung from him that bitter cry, *My God, my God, why hast thou forsaken me?* The injuries of an Enemy are easily born, but the forsakings of a Father are intolerable...

IV. Let us consider *How he suffered* all these things....1. He suffered *Innocently*; Isa. 53:9. *He had done no violence, neither was any deceit in his mouth; yet it pleased the Lord to bruise him.* 2 Cor. 5. 21. *He made him to be sin for us, who knew no sin*...2. He suffered all *Patiently*: Isa. 53. 7. *He was oppressed, and he was afflicted, yet he opened not his mouth, he is brought as a Lamb to the slaughter; and as a sheep before her shearers is dumb, so he openeth not his mouth*...3. Which is yet a higher step, he suffered all this *Willingly and Cheerfully*, John 10. 18. *No man taketh my Life from me, but I lay it down of my self*...

V. Let us consider, *For whom he suffered* all this. 1. *The Persons* for whom he suffered *deserved it not:* The expressions of the Scripture are full in this, Rom. 5. 7,8. *Peradventure for a Good man some would even dare to dye; but God commendeth his love towards us in that, while we were yet sinners, Christ died for us;* the objects upon which he looked upon in his sufferings were darkness, Eph. 5. 8. *Children of wrath,* Eph. 2. 3. *Aliens from the Common-wealth of Israel, strangers from the Covenant of Promise, having no hope, and without God in the world,* Eph. 2. 12. See but what a Monster the best of us were in our natural condition, when every power of our Soul and Body was quite corrupted from the use and end, for which they were made, Rom. 3. 9,10 &c. 2. As it was for those that deserved it not, nor any deliverance by it, so it was for a company of Creatures that *were no way folicitous* for, nor fought after redemption; such as were ignorant of their own Misery, and no ways endeavouring after Mercy. *Thus he was found of them that sought him not;* and surely little seeking could be found of such as were in such a condition, Eph. 2. 1. *Dead in Trespasses and Sins.* 3. Not only for those that neither deserved, nor sought after deliverance, but his sufferings were for those that were

Enemies; Rom. 5. 10. *If when we were Enemies, we were reconciled to God by the Death of his Son;* Col. 1. 21. *And you that were sometimes alienated and Enemies in your mind by wicked works, yet now hath he reconciled...*

VI. **From the consideration of the former particulars, it will easily appear what was the *Motive of this* great work.** We have seen in the creature nothing but Sin and Enmity against God, and consequently a just obligation to everlasting wrath and misery: So there we can find nothing that might upon any account of merit or desert draw out such mercy as this. We must seek for the motive in the *Author* of it: and in him there was *no Necessity* at all to bind him to it: It was his own free will that at first gave man a being, and blessed being; and when he had sinned against the Law and Conditions of his Creation, there was a Necessity of Justice for his Eternal Punishment, but no necessity at all for his Restitution. God made all things for his Glory, not because he stood in need of it; for he had in himself an infinite Self-sufficiency and Happiness, that stood not in need of the glory of his Creation, nor was capable of an accession by it: And if it had, yet the great God could have enjoyed the Glory of his Justice, in the everlasting punishment of unthankful man, and yet had glorious Creatures enough, the blessed Angels, to have been the everlasting partakers and admirers of his Goodness: And if there had been yet an absolute necessity of visible intellectual Creatures, to be the participants of his Goodness, and the active Instruments of his Glory; the same Power that created men, at first, could have created a new generation of man that might have supplied the defection of our first parents and their descendants. What then is the original of all his Goodness to poor sinful man? to purchase such a worthless creature at such an invaluable price as the blood of the Son of God? Nothing but Love; free undeserved Love; Love that loved before it was sought; that loved when it was rejected: Deut. 7. 7. *The Lord did not set his love upon you, nor choose you, because ye were more;* but because the Lord loved you: he loved you because he loved you: as Almighty God could not define himself by any thing but himself, *I am that I am,* Exod. 3. 14. so he can resolve his Love into no other motive than his Love; he loved you because he loved you: And here is the spring, the fountain of all this strange and unheard of Goodness of God in Christ; nothing but the free Love of God; John 3. 16. *So God loved the world that he gave his only begotten son,* &c. I John 4. 10. *Here is Love, not that we loved God, but that he loved us, and sent his Son to be a propitiation for our sins;* and that very same individual Love that was in the Father to send, was in the Son to come, and to die for us...

In reference to Man: And so the ends of our Lords suffering were principally these...To restore us to a most sure, everlasting and blessed Inheritance in Heaven. Gal. 4. 7. *If a Son, then an Heir of God through Christ:* and here is the complement of all; not only absolved from the guilt of sin, but reconciled to God, put into the relation of a Child of God; but after all this, to be everlastingly and unchangeable stated in a blessed condition unto all Eternity: and all this from the condition of a most vile, sinful lost Creature, and by such a price as the Blood of Christ. More need not, cannot be said...

Sitting Room at Mount Vernon

Mrs. Washington pauses a moment and looks about the room. She catches your gaze as she reverently closes her worn volume with a gleam in her eye and a look of peace on her countenance. You look away out the sitting-room window and see the noon sun gleaming off the sundial in the garden as you hear the hall time-piece sounding the hour. You sense the urgency of its message. You must focus; focus on eternity. George Washington's mother did, will you?

Mary Washington's Home in Fredericksburg, VA

Sundial in Her Backyard

DR. CHUCK HARDING
Missionary Evangelist

Growing up in the Washington D.C. area gave Dr. Chuck Harding a good understanding of our government and a love for history. God provided him the privilege of being the Deputy Commander of the Uniformed Protective Branch for the Diplomatic Security Service at the U.S. State Department. He is the founder of Awake America, which provides spiritual support to Capitol Hill and sponsors the Capitol Connection. He preaches God and Country meetings and Constitutional Awareness Conferences throughout the United States.

PASTOR T. MICHAEL CREED
Independent Baptist Church

Pastor T. Michael Creed grew up in a pastor's home in the greater Washington D.C. area. He has pastored the Independent Baptist Church of Clinton, Maryland for 22 years and has a desire to reach Capitol Hill for Christ. He has teamed up with Dr. Harding in an effort to help churches better understand the need for their involvement in governmental affairs.